THE UNITED METHODIST CLERGY
BOOK *of*

Firsts

F. BELTON JOYNER JR.

The United Methodist Clergy Book of Firsts

The General Board of Higher Education and Ministry leads and serves The United Methodist Church in the recruitment, preparation, nurture, education, and support of Christian leaders—lay and clergy—for the work of making disciples of Jesus Christ for the transformation of the world. The General Board of Higher Education and Ministry of The United Methodist Church serves as an advocate for the intellectual life of the church. The Board's mission embodies the Wesleyan tradition of commitment to the education of laypersons and ordained persons by providing access to higher education for all persons.

The Wesley's Foundery Books is named for the abandoned foundery that early followers of John Wesley transformed into a church, which became the cradle of London's Methodist movement.

The United Methodist Clergy Book of Firsts

HIGHER EDUCATION & MINISTRY
General Board of Higher Education and Ministry
THE UNITED METHODIST CHURCH

Contents

To the students I have had in three decades of teaching in the Course of Study School.

Introduction

It was moving day. All across the annual conference, district superintendents were hopping into their cars and driving from town to town, from rural village to rural village, from parsonage to parsonage to visit pastors who were about to begin ministry in new places.

So, the D.S. pulled into the crowded backyard next door to Middleton United Methodist Church. It would appear that half the congregation had turned out to welcome Chip Graham, their new preacher. Helpful women and men took turns hauling boxes off the large moving truck. Alice Martin was heard muttering, "If this fellow is just starting divinity school, why does he already have so many heavy boxes filled with all these books?" Mild complaints were standard fare for Alice.

Indeed, Chip Graham was about to launch his four years in seminary. His career as an accountant was behind him and his new life as a pastor awaited him. His usual self-confidence seemed to have taken a hiatus. All these new people! All this new place! All this uncertainty!

As the district superintendent made her way through the parsonage of Middleton Church, she nodded in greeting at church leaders she had seen from time to time at charge conference or at district gatherings. It was always a disadvantage when everyone recognized her and she barely recognized a face, much less a name. Finally, she spotted Chip Graham and stepped over to speak to this new student pastor, now one of her colleagues.

"How's it going, Chip?"

"Oh, hey, Dr. Britt. I guess it is going OK. Kind of busy."

"I guess it is tough moving into a parsonage when you've had your own house for all these years."

"You are right about that. Marcia and I had a hard time deciding which things we ought to store and which things to bring."

One of the helpers said, "Preacher, where do you want this table?"

Chip made no response.

The question came a bit louder: "Preacher, where do you want me to put this table?"

No answer.

"PREACHER! WHERE SHOULD I PUT THIS TABLE?"

When Chip made no reply, the district superintendent tapped him on the shoulder. "Chip, I think this man is asking you a question."

Chip looked startled. "Oh! You are talking to me! No one has ever called me 'Preacher' before! I guess that's who I am now!"

––––––––––––––

This book is about those times that a first-time pastor faces a new identity. In some parts of the country, it is "Preacher." Somewhere else it might be "Reverend." Or maybe the term is "Pastor." Perhaps the title is "Sister" or "Brother." And, in some parts of the country, more than one new male United Methodist cleric has been greeted with "Father."

This book is about those times when:

- the pressures of new decisions show up,
- the first unwelcomed expectation appears,
- the initial encounter comes with "all those reports we have to turn in,"
- you find the pianist plays only from memory,
- the predecessor just won't let go, and
- you attempt to carve out a personal life in the midst of congregation schedules, community calendar, and sudden crises.

This book is about you.

As you will note from chapter headings, these issues always come in systematic, orderly fashion. (If you believe that, I have some beachfront property in Antarctica that I'd like to sell you.) All of these topics need to be addressed early on in your new appointment, probably even before you get there. "First Day" matters are really, really, really, really important for early attention. "First Week" issues are really, really, really important for your thinking. "First Month" questions are really, really important even before you move. "First Year" lists are really important for your pre-appointment consideration. Well, you get the idea.

Of course, there is a good chance that this book won't give you much help. You and I are different from each other. (For one thing, I am a Duke Blue Devils, St. Louis Cardinals, Carolina Panthers fan. What are you?) Our places of service won't always match up. (My first appointment when I was "straight out of the barrel" was to organize a new congregation: "You want me to do what?") We may not agree on appropriate pastoral roles and responsibilities. (I don't even always agree with myself.) You and I may have dissimilar gifts. (For example, do you even know what dartball is?) We may find our joy in dissimilar places. (My choice: Brussels sprout casserole or free tickets to the big game. Hmmm.) And there is the truth that neither you nor I can anticipate every "first" that either God or the devil will put on the plate.

But it is important that we talk about it. Some of it will be surprising joys; some of it will be disappointing hurts; some of it will be mind-deadening boredom; some of it will be mystery; some of it will be "won't know until later." All of it will be ministry. So, let's begin the conversation. And be thinking about where you want the fellow to put that table.

The First Day

When Trevor Barber hung up the phone, he was not sure what he should do next. Grab a map? Look for some information online? Call his wife? Kneel in prayer? All he had said to the caller was, "Yes. Thank you, Mr. Alvarez. I look forward to having—what did you call it?—a covenant visit." He had never heard of Glosson Memorial United Methodist Church; he had little sense of where it was and now he was going to be the pastor there: a real pastor with real people. No more imagining what it would be like. It was time to find out for sure.

Your First Appointment

How did you find out that you were going to have an appointment (¶ 428.3)? It might have been a phone call from a district superintendent. It might have been a face-to-face conversation or an e-mail. There is a good chance that you were told: "Don't tell anyone except your family." What? This is one of the biggest moments of your life and you are supposed to keep it quiet?

Why this injunction not to share the good news about the appointment? After exhaustive research, I discovered that 96.7 percent of appointments end up being just what the bishop and cabinet first decided. But what about the other 3.3 percent (¶ 428.8)? Think about it: If things change, do you want to go to serve a church that thinks you are a second or third choice? Think about it: What disappointments and hurts happen when you have to wrap your heart and mind around some new reality? Think about it: Might announcing appointment decisions prematurely limit the flexibility the bishop and cabinet need to make the best possible matches? (OK. I made up that "96.7 percent" statistic, but everything else in this book is absolutely true.)

At the other end of the appointment, there has been a call or a meeting or an e-mail to let the Pastor-Parish Relations Committee (PPRC) or Staff-Parish Relations Committee (SPRC) know that you are coming (¶ 428.3). United Methodist congregations are accustomed to pastors coming and going, so very likely this is not the first time they have gone through a pastoral change. What might be super-new for you may well be routine for them. (What differences does that make?)

In some annual conferences, there is a set time for going public with appointment information. For example, on the first Sunday in May, the PPRC chair in every local church will tell the congregation who will be its pastor for the next year. Or, in other settings, there may be a delay until the bishop and cabinet have made all the appointments. Or, there may be no barrier to standing on the street corner and proclaiming, "I'm the new pastor at Pork City."

 Here's an idea: Ask your district superintendent when you can tell others about your appointment.

Prayer: Lord Jesus, thank you for this affirmation of my call. Amen.

Linda Barber-Carpenter was thrilled about her first appointment. By going to weekend Course of Study classes spread throughout the year, she would be able to keep her part-time job at the Dawson County Public Library and still give half-time service at Otterbein Memorial United Methodist Church. "I can't wait to get over there and meet those people. I can't wait to drive over there out in the country and find that church!"

Introductions at New Appointment

This is what I was told after getting the word that I was moving to another church: "Now don't go over there and look around. That's not your place yet. We'll arrange for someone to show you around after the introductory visit." Then, there was a pause, and my district superintendent lowered his voice almost in a conspiratorial way. "Now, Belton, I know you are going to go over there even though I said not to, so make sure you go at night and drive down the street with your car lights turned off. Don't let anybody see you!" (The rest of the story: My wife, Toni, and I drove over in the daytime. We avoided eye contact with any people on the sidewalk. And, oh, by the way, the appointment got changed, and we ended up at a place we didn't see until our "official" visit!)

Official visit? In some annual conferences, there is a tradition of introductory visits. These may be called "covenant visits" or "welcome meetings" or "connecting the connection." What they are not—and this is important—what they are not is a job interview. This is not an occasion for a congregation to say yes or no to the pending appointment. This is not so the incoming pastor can make a judgment about whether this is a desirable appointment. This meeting, usually with just the Pastor-Parish Relations Committee, is designed for "get acquainted" and to resolve any lingering practical matters related to the move.

Often, the district superintendent or the D.S.'s representative will schedule and preside at the session. In other settings, you (and perhaps family) will "go on your own" to the new place of ministry. Seldom would it be appropriate for the departing pastor to be present. If there is a parsonage, that pastor may invite you to tour the house, but keep in mind that it is still that pastor's home. (Parsonage matters show up later in this book.) You should get a chance to walk through the church building.

What would be appropriate attire for such an occasion? I dare not give sartorial advice, but keep in mind that you are making a first impression. Is there such a thing as "business casual"? This is probably not a good time to wear your tennis outfit. If you are unsure, just ask your district superintendent what kind of setting this will be. (Will there be a meal? A picnic?)

If you are married, most congregations would probably like to meet your spouse. There probably won't be provisions for child care, so keep that in mind in deciding whom to pile into the car.

Doing a little homework will help you get ready for this introductory time. Do the church or churches have a website? What can you find out there? Is there a history? Find conference journals, either online on the annual conference website or in print editions (sometimes in church libraries). Look at the statistical data, usually in the back of the journal. (The following numbers in parentheses refer to the answers given in Table I, Table II, and Table III, usually at the back of the journal. These numbers do not stay the same from time to time (¶ 807.16), but, hey, it's a start! Later in this book, we'll explore how to prepare your own reports.) What is the trend in average worship attendance (10)? How often is there a profession of faith (2a, 2b)? What evidence is there of missional or social involvement (30, 40, 41, 42)? How diverse is the congregation (9a, b, c, d, e, f, g, h)? On a multi-point charge, is one congregation statistically very different from the other(s)? What is the record on paying connectional apportionments (35a, 35b)? How many deaths occurred last year (8)? There are over fifty categories in Table I, Table II, and Table III. There is a lot of information there to stir your thinking! In addition to these data, you might check to see how long the present pastor has been there; it would also be helpful to dig through previous journals so you can determine how often they have had a pastoral change.

What kinds of questions might the PPRC have for you (¶ 427.2)? Here are some I have heard. Where are you from originally? Tell us about your call to preach. Do you plan to wear a robe? What do you think about homosexuality? Do you like to visit? Does your spouse sing in the choir? Are you going to try to preach politics? What's your favorite book of the Bible? When were you saved? What did you do before you became a pastor? How many children do you have? What would you like to know about us? What do you think about having an American flag in the sanctuary? Do you have anything against our holding a church raffle? What do you like to do when you have free time? (Don't worry! You probably won't get all of these "get-acquainted" inquiries!)

And you would do well to think of some questions for the PPRC (¶ 427.1). In the community, what is this church best known for (¶ 427.3)? When were the "best years" for this congregation? What are the nearest other United Methodist churches and what do you do together? How do you get along with nearby churches of other denominations? Do you have a pictorial directory? What are three things I need to do when I first get here? What is the general attitude toward the conference? What's one thing you hope I won't do? What are some examples of "your prayers, your presence, your gifts, your service, and your witness"? (Those terms are part of the vows taken when one is received into the membership of a local church; for example, see no. 38 of *The United Methodist Hymnal.* "Your witness" was added by the 2008 General Conference, so it may not be printed in hymn-books older than that.) If this is a cross-racial or cross-cultural appointment, how do we find grace in this "elephant in the room"? Who is the lay member that I shall probably see at annual conference?

There are some practical questions that might best be addressed in private conversation or perhaps be raised by someone other than you. What time can I show up on Moving Day? (In some annual conferences, there is a tradition of "one out by noon, another in at 1:00.") When do I get paid? (Is this a flexible arrangement?) How much is budgeted for the pastor's continuing education? Is everything clear about reimbursement for travel expenses? If there is a parsonage, whom do I call if there is a problem?

 Here's an idea: Make a list of things you want to find out at the introductory visit.

Prayer: Calm my spirit, Lord, as I journey into new places. Amen.

Isao Jung looked at the calendar, about the only thing not yet packed for the upcoming move. "Wow! In eight days, I'll be preaching and praying at Hope Church! I hope we'll sing 'Surely the Presence of the Lord.' That's my favorite! And I hope there will be a layperson to read the Scripture lessons. And I wonder if the lay member of annual conference will be making a report. How do I find out all this?"

First Worship Service

Oops! It could fall through the cracks in this time of transition: Who will plan the worship for that first Sunday? It makes sense for you to do it because you are going to be the pastor. It makes sense for your predecessor to do it because that pastor knows the local ropes. It makes sense for a local church planning team to do it because they will be living with the results. See how simple this is? Hmmm.

Talk with your predecessor to make sure "who is going to do what." Are you planning the service or is someone else? Whom do you wish to preside? How about an introduction of you by the chair of the Pastor-Parish Relations Committee? Do you have a copy of the order of service from some recent Sundays? If there is a bulletin or projected material, who prepares that? What is the deadline? Because you are not yet the pastor, ask permission from your predecessor to connect with worship leaders: musicians, ushers, liturgists, someone who makes announcements, et al. (Of course, if you want to have a good time at someone else's expense, wait until just before the service to tell the liturgist that you want Matthew 1:1-17 as the text to be read. Zerubbabel? Jehoshaphat? Next!) Last minute surprises do not make for comfortable leadership; the Holy Spirit will provide enough fresh flames; there is no need for you to fumble your way to the unexpected.

Some of the issues addressed here probably do not apply if you are being appointed to a multiple-staff situation (¶ 428.5c). In those settings, there may be other kinds of "first day" issues. When does the staff meet? To whom am I accountable? How do we "cover" for each other as backup? What adjective would best describe relationships within the staff?

In the next section, we can chat a bit about the first sermon in your appointment.

 Here's an idea: Work with your predecessor to make certain all is in readiness for your first Sunday.

Prayer: Eternal, life-giving God, keep me reminded that you are the focus of life within the journey, and I am not. Amen.

The First Week

Ernie Hemingway was worried about moving to Vernon City. It was something that happened every time he was in a new setting: "Is your name really Ernest Hemingway?" Then, there would be a pause followed by the same joke he had heard two dozen times: "You don't look dead!" He knew he would smile as if to say: "How clever!" and then move on to the business at hand: How do I go about getting around in a place where I have not lived? What should my first sermon be about? Which hospital do these folks usually go to? What do I do if my predecessor wants to store "a few things" at the parsonage? Whom can I trust to give me the straight scoop? By then, you might be thinking: Is this what Jesus had in mind when he called me to preach?

More on First Worship Service

It sounds simple: "preach the Word of God" (¶ 340.2a[1]). Let me try a rather clumsy metaphor: The destination might be certain, but what vehicle is best for getting there—car, truck, bus, train, plane, feet? Chasing down answers to these questions might help you on that first Sunday. Do you stay in the pulpit when you preach or do you move around? Is there a sound system? Who operates it? Do you wear a microphone? Is the sermon being recorded? Is there a Bible on the pulpit? Can the height of the pulpit be adjusted if your four-foot-eleven or six-foot-seven frame calls for it? How do the offering plates end up in the hands of the ushers? What happens when the offering is brought forward?

Sometime beforehand, walk through that first service, preferably in the worship space. Where will you be at each moment in the service? Where do you go after the benediction? (For that matter, when and how do you enter the worship space?) If you are serving a multi-point charge, what happens if you are early/late getting from one congregation to the next?

What about these things if they seem not to matter much? The kingdom will not screech to a halt if you just stand there waiting for the pianist to start playing the next hymn while the pianist is determined not to play until you announce the hymn number "like we've always done." (I doubt that many will use that time of expectant silence for prayer!) However, if you are not a little bit nervous at this first service, you might consider that you are not taking things seriously enough!

Very few first-time pastors have been run out of town because they did not have a match, failing to realize that they were expected to have a way to ignite the acolyte's candlelighter. Not many clergy were deemed heathen because no one told them they were supposed to have pre-service prayer with the choir. Seldom is a young pastor told—oh, yes; it actually happened to me—by the wife of the district superintendent: "You should not wear argyle socks in the pulpit." However, if you have not given some thought to these small things, some will hesitate to turn you loose on larger things. (Did I just hear someone reading Luke 16:10?)

 Here's an idea: If possible, walk through the worship service in the space where it will take place.

Prayer: Come, Holy Spirit, bring the freshness of your presence. Amen.

The computer screen was still blank. For some time, Elaine McAllister had been pondering her first sermon at Asbury Heights United Methodist Church. Tell my personal faith story? Follow the lectionary? Use something I've done before? Memorize? Use notes? Write a full manuscript or just an outline? What does God want said in this situation? Focus on the Fourth of July or ignore the fact that a civic holiday happens to be my first Sunday? Borrow from something I find online? She reached for the keyboard and began typing: "I've dreamed of this moment for years. I get to preach as the pastor of my own congregation." She hit the delete button and erased "my own congregation" and she changed it to "I get to preach as the pastor of this gathering of Christ's people." She paused and then she added: "But now that I am here, I'm not sure what I should say." After a minute of staring at the screen, she turned off her computer.

First Sermon

Thank goodness that Elaine McAllister had trouble putting together that first sermon! When we become casual about our preaching, we have opened the door to a sense that maybe this is not really very important. God forbid!

A sermon should grow out of Scripture. Some congregations and some pastors have found that the best way to do this while being addressed by "the whole message of Scripture" is to follow the "Revised Common Lectionary," a three-year cycle of readings from the Old Testament, Psalter, Epistles, and Gospels. (You can find these on pp. 227–37 of *The United Methodist Book of Worship*.)

One reason to use the lectionary is that it expands your congregational community to include all those other congregations (both United Methodist and other denominations) who are also drawing from the same biblical well on the same Sunday. Clergy often get together in lectionary study groups to join their insights as they prepare to preach from the same texts. The lectionary moves in a systematic way so all the notes of the good news get played.

Is it easy to be guided by the lectionary? No. One time I was asked to teach a course on using the lectionary in unusual situations. I made up strange circumstances and a class member had to prepare and deliver a sermon—based on the lection for that Sunday—that would "work" for that setting. My two favorite make-believe situations were (1) the Sunday after the parsonage burned down and most of the members blamed the pastor's children for setting the fire and (2) the first Sunday after the congregation divided because the pastor refused to hold a dog's funeral in the sanctuary.

The lectionary will sometimes send us to unexpected places. (That sounds like the Holy Spirit, doesn't it?) But, truth to tell, there are times when a preacher would have to manipulate the text in order to "make it fit." For this reason, there are times when even the most "lectionary-committed" pastor will choose to explore some other scriptural truth. Perhaps even worse than having no biblical basis for what I preach is fudging on what a passage says in order to make the point I want to make.

Another option, of course, is to pick your own text for your sermon. Some preachers prefer this approach as a way of matching congregational needs with relevant biblical texts. This may lead you to a topical series. Although there is a risk of staying with favorite or "easy" scriptures, this method may allow for greater energy and assurance in your preaching.

Is it too soon to plan ahead? As you anticipate how your preaching may develop over the coming months, start a file of ideas, illustrations, and points to be made when it is time to preach on a particular text.

If you have a manuscript or extensive notes, start a file of your sermons. This not only creates something to draw from for emergency use, it gives some fodder for your future reflection on your preaching emphases. At some point, it could even help you avoid careless repetition. Some pastors maintain such a filing system with the sermons in alphabetical order by title. Others prefer to organize the sermons by their biblical text, in the order in which the text appears in the Scripture. A few simply add the sermons into a box in the chronological order of when preached. A less effective plan is to dump them into a bag "to be sorted later"! Of course, print copies and digital copies will have their own different requirements for storage.

After you have been preaching for a while at the same congregation, ask your Pastor-Parish Relations Committee this question: "What do you think is the main theme of my preaching?" When I have asked that, I have sometimes found out that what I thought I was saying was not what was being heard.

Here's an idea: Put into one sentence what you think the biblical text for your sermon is saying.

*Prayer: Precious Lord, open my mouth so what
I speak will be your Word. Amen.*

"We have to go to a district meeting this very first week? With all else we have going on, the last thing we need is to trot off a couple of hours away to some meeting the district superintendent thinks is important!" Logan and LaNilta Johnson, a newly appointed clergy couple, were bemoaning the "command performance" nature of this district gathering of clergy who were about to move. Logan was assigned to Furman United Methodist Church; LaNilta was to be the associate at Steeple City United Methodist Church. There was a parsonage for the associate at Steeple City UMC, so that is where the couple would be living (albeit amidst boxes and turmoil). Ugh! Now, this district waste of time!

Let's suppose that on the way home from the meeting, LaNilta is driving and Logan is reading aloud some of the materials handed out at the session for newly appointed pastors.

"Did you know that some states do not have a state income tax? And here's something I had not thought about. State and federal income taxes are different in some ways for clergy. For example, it says that under Internal Revenue Service code, section 107, we can exclude from our taxable income anything we spend on furnishings that we buy for the parsonage. And, if we pay the utilities, we can leave that amount out of our taxable income. And we'll want personal property insurance on our things at the parsonage. If I am reading this thing right, we can exclude the cost of that insurance from our taxable income. It's even more confusing if we were living in our own place or renting a house! And some of this applies to income tax but not to Social Security. Good grief! As soon as we get home, I'm going to set up an appointment with Jackson Turner. I know he has helped us with our tax filing before, but I want to make sure we don't miss out on something. We'll never be able to remember all this next spring! We need to start keeping records now, so we'll have the correct information when it is time to file next April!"

 Here's an idea: Go to Cokesbury.com and order the current edition of *Minister's Tax & Financial Guide*, published by Zondervan each year.

Prayer: Help me, dear God, find the right path for rendering unto Caesar, so I do my share. Amen.

Clergy Income Tax

Tax laws are constantly under review. What might be true as I type these words might not be true when you read these words! Consult with colleagues about their own experiences in developing fair and accurate tax returns. I have a friend who told me about an accountant who had taken the trouble to master the intricacies of United Methodist clergy tax filing. Getting to this accountant's office is well worth the drive across several counties to get there!

Moving Expenses

What about your moving expenses? If the church has paid some of those expenses, they might be deductible from gross income. The provisions for deducting for moving expenses are pretty tight. How far did you move? (At one time, you had to move at least fifty miles to your new place of work for it to count.) When did you move? Did your job actually require you to move? Did you stop for a cheeseburger while you were moving? (Meals while moving are not deductible.) The mileage rate for these moving expenses deductions changes from time to time. If you think this is getting complicated, enjoy the thought that there are additional provisions for each of the fifty states, the District of Columbia, and Puerto Rico. Are we having fun yet?

 Here's an idea: Keep careful record of all expenses related to your move; you can determine later if they are deductible expenses.

Prayer: You have traveled with me on all of my life journey, Holy Spirit, so I give thanks for your presence as I make this transition. Amen.

Travel Expenses

Guidelines for travel expenses vary from conference to conference. Such costs may be reimbursed or, if not, can be deducted for tax purposes. Obviously, the travel needs to be related to the work of ministry. (When we drove from North Carolina to New Jersey to visit my mother-in-law, I suggested that if I asked the blessing at the supper table in New Jersey, I could count that family travel as a business expense. Jesus convinced me that I was wrong. I prayed anyhow.)

Start keeping records of your clergy travel now! The information you maintain is supposed to be contemporaneous, not retroactive. Keep a mileage record (notebook, tablet, phone, for example) in your car and make notes after each episode.

Of course, clergy, like other citizens, can make deductions for charitable, nonprofit contributions. This includes both monetary gifts and travel for voluntary work. Take care! So much of the ministry and outreach of a church is nonprofit helping that it is easy to let your travel for work bleed over into "gifts to charity." Is driving to that Habitat for Humanity project expense you have as a pastor, or is it an expense you have as a volunteer? If you take a homeless man to a shelter twenty miles away, is that pastoral travel, or is that volunteering on behalf of the shelter? If you carry the unsold items from a church yard sale to the Goodwill store in the next town, is that a church-related expense, or is that your own gift to charity? These are the simple questions. Just wait until the difficult ones arise.

 Here's an idea: Put down this book and grab your phone; call your tax advisor and set up an appointment. (Uh, then pick up the book again.)

Prayer: Good Shepherd, right now I need your peace that passes understanding. Amen.

Fees with Weddings and Funerals

Would you like to start an interesting fight at the next pastors' meeting? If you have EMTs available, go ahead and ask: Should a pastor accept a fee for doing a wedding or for conducting a funeral? Our clergy colleagues often have, shall we say, strong opinions on that subject.

"You idiot! Those people are just taking advantage of you, using up your free Saturday, plus all the counseling time you had with that couple who will never set foot in the church!"

"What kind of mercenary fool are you? If counseling and leading worship at weddings and at funerals is not part of your pastoral ministry, then I don't understand ministry. Why are you double-dipping?"

"You know as well as I do that my salary is set so low because the people at the church count on my picking up a few extra dollars with this extra work."

"Why don't you start charging visitors who come to the Communion table? I don't see any difference between doing that and collecting an honorarium for burying the dead if they are not members of your church!"

Uh, you will have to sort through your options and decide how best to live out your understanding of your role as pastor. (See a recommendation on p. 139 of *The United Methodist Book of Worship.*) I put this item in an early chapter because it will serve you well to decide in advance how you will answer the question: "Well, Pastor, how much will we owe you for doing this wedding?"

 Here's an idea: The next time there are three or four pastors together, risk bringing up this issue of whether or not to accept fees for weddings and funerals.

Prayer: Creator God, you called me to this ministry; please hold my hand and my heart as I struggle with what all that means. Amen.

Other Tax Matters and Property Insurance

There are multiple additional issues related to clergy taxation. For example, there can be deductions for educational expenses; however—and it is a big "however"—if those expenses are incurred in meeting the minimum educational requirements of The United Methodist Church, they are not deductible.

And what constitutes a business expense? Cell phone? Office space in your own home? Half the cost of meals at annual conference (because you are required to attend)? Subscription to religious journals? Membership in a club where you get to meet potential members? Treating a colleague to lunch when planning a joint Good Friday service? Cost of getting your robe cleaned? Your desktop computer that is used 49 percent of the time for church work? (OK. That is a sneaky question; the break point is 50 percent.) No matter how you and your tax advisor decide on these questions, you will need documentation. So, start saving those receipts and canceled checks!

If you are living in your own house (rather than church-provided housing), the tax consequences are different. For example, a housing allowance given to you by the church can be left out of your taxable income, only to the extent that it is less than the fair rental value of your housing. You also have to keep track of actual housing expenses, and you cannot exclude from taxable income any amount of the housing allowance that exceeds actual expenses.

By the way, if you are living in a parsonage or in rental housing, be aware that you need to take renter's insurance on your personal property. (If you are in your own house, you probably already have property insurance . . . uh, don't you?) Renter's insurance is not terribly expensive and is well worth the investment for protection against the kinds of losses that can suddenly appear. (I still remember my high school son calling from the parsonage and saying, "Dad, you may want to come home. Sometime while we were all gone, the ceiling in the dining room collapsed.")

I know my head is swimming after thinking about these tax things. Swimming is one thing, but drowning is another, so I believe I best move to another topic!

 Here's an idea: Go, take a nap!

Prayer: Master, when I plow into new and difficult territory, grant me patience and openness and peace. Amen.

Ronnie Birmingham called out to his wife. She was in the next room, busily packing the towels, washcloths, and other things they would want to get to quickly once they completed the move to the parsonage for the Harbor-Clearview Charge. "Honey, did you put Perky's dog food in the box labeled 'garage' or the box labeled 'kitchen?'" Perky was the eponymously named German shepherd who had been a wedding gift four years ago.

Family Pet at Parsonage

Uh, oh! The good folks at Harbor-Clearview once had a pastor whose cat had clawed scratches on all the furniture in the parsonage and whose litter box was more litter than box. They had decided "No more pets in the parsonage." So, now it is time for Robbie, Barbara, and Perky to show up.

In another book I wrote (*Life in the Fish Bowl: Everyday Challenges of Pastors and Their Families* (Nashville: Abingdon Press, 2006), I suggested thirty possibilities for handling situations similar to that in which the Birminghams now find themselves. With the kind permission of the team at Abingdon Press, I quote those options here (with an occasional update).

(1) Find a new home for the pet; (2) provide backyard facilities for the animal; (3) agree on limited pet access within the house; (4) find someone who will keep the pet until you are living elsewhere; (5) keep the pet in a pen, even if in the house; (6) replace all flea-bearing critters with things that have fins; (7) train your pet to bite any visitors; (8) allow the animal(s) inside only at night or in cases of dangerous weather; (9) make a security deposit against damages; (10) sign a statement agreeing to leave the parsonage as you found it (or better); (11) ask for third-party intervention; (12) have the cat's claws deactivated (may not be legal or recommended even for indoor cats); (13) explain to your pet that you are leaving the ordained ministry because of fleas; (14) find a pet lover in the congregation who will help others in the congregation understand that pets do not destroy a house; (15) have a letter from your previous congregation (or rental agency) indicating that your guinea pig actually improved the property value of the house; (16) offer to have a six-month trial period with your pet(s) in the parsonage; (17) point out that if the pet armadillo cannot come, your family will not come; (18) keep your pet cocker spaniel at the church, saying, "We have to keep Brownie at the church because you will not allow her to be at the parsonage"; (19) make sure that the no-pets policy applies to the pet you have—bird in a cage, fish in a bowl, cricket in a cage, and so forth; (20) say no to the assignment; (21) show the parsonage committee a picture of Jesus holding a baby lamb; (22) get the advice of your Pastor-Parish Relations Committee or Pastoral Advisory Committee; (23) invite parsonage committee members to see the arrangements you have made for your pet at the parsonage; (24) be clear as to the source and rationale for the no pets policy; (25) have your ten-year-old daughter (tissues in hand) appeal to the recalcitrant committee; (26) at the peril of creating an unsealable fissure in church life, ignore the policy; (27) ask how most pet owners in the

community handle their pets; (28) discuss what ought to be (and will be) off-limits for the pet; (29) explain your pet's previous history of behavior as a house pet; (30) offer to exchange your dog for a pet buffalo.

Obviously, some of these, uh, suggestions are more useful than others. However you work out these matters, keep in mind that when you move from the parsonage, you will want to arrange for a professional cleaner and pest control expert to make sure that your successor "inherits" a pet-free house.

 Here's an idea: Talk with your predecessor about experiences related to pets at the parsonage.

Prayer: Creator and lover of all you have created, I want to glorify you in all the family decisions we make. Amen.

"Why the funeral director?" Cynthia Apisai wondered aloud. As she and Lois Barber drank coffee and compared notes on getting moved to their first appointments, Cynthia said, "At least that's what Ernesto Perez told me to do. He's in his third appointment, so I figure he knows something about getting connected in a new community. But the funeral director? Why?"

First Visits

The boxes are still cluttering the hallway, but it is time to start being "pastoral." How does a fresh-in-town pastor get started in visitation and meeting people and getting known? In most places, the door-to-door scenario is unlikely. So, whom do I see first?

In many annual conferences, a departing pastor leaves a list of folks who need an early visit. Has someone recently had a death in the family? Who is in the hospital or just home from surgery? Is there a new baby in the congregation? Are there key leaders with whom to touch base? What about shut-ins who depend on the pastor to keep them connected? Has a family just moved to the community? These are good connections for early visits. Ministry is about surprises, so new situations and circumstances will adjust your best-made plans for early visitation.

But what about the funeral director? (Also called a mortician or an undertaker or an embalmer.) Sooner or later, you are going to be working in a professional relationship with the funeral director. Both of you will be dealing with families in times of crisis, of loss, of relief, of despair, of anger, of division, of joy, of dependency, of courage, of shock, of almost any human emotion that you can imagine (and perhaps some you cannot). Getting to know each other before having to work together will be helpful. Your roles are indeed different and without question you, as pastor, are in charge of the worship experience. Almost every funeral director understands that. An awareness that you can count on each other in these times of service will give both of you a place of harmony in a time that otherwise can be stressful.

If there are multiple funeral homes (mortuaries) nearby, members of the church can indicate the ones most frequently used by parishioners. A tour of the funeral home facilities will help you avoid surprises when there is going to be a service held at the mortuary. For example, where does the pastor go when arriving for a service? Where will people be gathering for a visitation (or wake, as it is sometimes called)? Some families appreciate the pastor accompanying them when they go to make plans at the funeral home or when they are choosing a casket or when they are deciding about music. You will feel more comfortable in those roles if you have seen the layout and met the personnel at the funeral home.

 Here's an idea: Make a list of the persons and places you will visit within the first two or three weeks.

Prayer: Lord Jesus, you went into homes and places of business as well as worship spaces. Go with me now in these connections that are new to me. Amen.

"The last time I was in the hospital," Charles Jung said, "was when I was born." Charles was picking the brain of a more experienced clergyperson. "What do I need to know about hospital visiting? I figure that will be something I'll be doing almost as soon as I get there."

Hospital Ministry

Charles Jung is correct. There are illnesses. There are surgeries. There are births. There are accidents. There are tests. There are procedures. There are false alarms and there are waits at the emergency room. Yes, you and the hospital will get to be well acquainted. And the "get-acquainted" occasion may well be one of the first ministries of your appointment. (¶ 340.2a[4])

If you are newly appointed, there is a good chance that the patient will not know you. Introduce yourself! And, if someone has asked you to visit "my cousin twice removed on my mother's side," there is a possibility that the cousin does not expect and perhaps does not wish to see you. Grace and graciousness are two different gifts, but these would be good times for both!

Do you know which hospitals folks from your parish usually go to? Is there a nearby facility for "ordinary things" and a major medical center farther away for "big things"?

Where do you park when you get to the hospital? At some sites, you are on your own. Other places have reserved free parking for clergy. You might be required to get a clergy parking permit. The person at the information desk (usually in the main lobby) can direct you to the proper office. Of course, you might have to pay for parking when making hospital visits. Here is one for your late-at-night conscience struggles: "Do I use my free clergy parking if I am visiting my own grandmother at the hospital? What if she is a member of the church I serve? Is there something spiritually wrong with me if this question does not bother me at all?"

Should you have a prayer with every patient you visit at the hospital? I recall dropping by to see a member who was in the hospital "for observation." As I got ready to leave, I said, "Let's have a prayer." To my surprise, she panicked and exclaimed, "Oh, I had no idea that my situation was that bad!" Then, I remember a teacher of mine who said, "It is better to think later that you wish you had not had a prayer than to think later I wish I had said a prayer." Most patients will be grateful for your prayers. If there is hospital staff or perhaps another patient in the room, alert them to your prayer time. There might be a rare circumstance when the best you can do is to have silent prayer.

OK. I can't resist. I want to tell you about one hospital prayer I offered. Late one night, I was called to go to the hospital where one of my members was threatening nurses and doctors and security with a broad knife he had somehow secured. "We think he will listen to you, Preacher," the caller said. When I got to the room, although my member still held the knife firmly, he greeted me warmly. We chatted for a while as I rambled through every topic I could think of. All seemed to be calming down. So, I said, "Would you like to have a prayer together?" "Oh, yes," he said. Then he added, "If you don't mind, Reverend, I'm going to keep my eyes open as we pray. Otherwise, they may try to take my knife away from me while my eyes are closed." (The story does have a happy ending: he eventually fell asleep and the quick-moving attendant took the weapon.)

Do you have a pocket-sized Bible or an online version? Some pastors like to have such an edition with them, especially when doing hospital ministry, in case either the patient or the family want to hear a scripture passage appropriate to the moment.

Somewhere along the way, you are likely to end up at the hospital at some unusual hour and find the door locked. It is a security issue for some sites. Check for some sign that will direct you to an open door. When in doubt, go to the emergency room entrance. Someone there can help you. Over time you will learn the best hours for making your hospital rounds. Some units do not allow visitations except during certain hours, but that is not likely to apply to clergy. Nevertheless, unless it is an emergency or unusual circumstance, you might honor those hours.

Hospital visits are not usually an occasion for lingering conversation. After all, there is a reason this person is in the hospital! I have a friend who always sits down when he is in the hospital room; he stays no longer than he would if he were standing up, but he says his sitting communicates to the patient that the pastor is not rushing. For some patients, your visit is a link to the outside world. You probably ought to check with the patient (or family member) to find out whether "It's OK to share what you've told me" or "I'd rather everyone not know that." (¶ 340.2a[5])

Check with the hospital to see if they prefer pastors to wear clergy badges. In some cultures, it is appropriate for you to wear a clerical collar. These identifying marks may give you access to some otherwise off-limits areas such as Intensive Care Units.

The patients are not the only ones who need pastoral attention. Is there a family member trembling with anxiety in the waiting room? A "thanks for your work" comment to members of the hospital staff may well make someone's day. And it is not unheard of for an unrelated stranger to recognize that you are a pastor and ask you for "just a moment of your time." Sadly, you may be there as devastating news is brought to a waiting family.

There is something about a hospital that increases the emotional component of situations and relationships. Extra uncertainty. Extra joy. Extra dismay. Extra doubt. Extra faith. Extra sadness. Extra need. Extra sacrifice. Extra extra. And you, the pastor, are called to be the non-anxious presence.

 Here's an idea: Each time you get parked at the hospital, think over what awaits you and offer it all to God in prayer.

Prayer: Remind me, O Lord, that your love has preceded me to every place. Amen.

"Well," Harold Glosson said to his new pastor, Ruben Guillermo, "I've never heard you preach, but you are bound to be better than that woman we had here before you. She never looked up from whatever it was she was reading from the pulpit." Ruben, making his first home visits after becoming pastor at Glosson Memorial United Methodist Church, remembered what Greg Glosson, Harold's brother, had told him: "We've had lots of preachers here at this church, but I'll tell you that Linda Perkins was the best one we ever had for knowing the Bible. She took the Word seriously and prepared carefully. I loved her preaching." In his mind, Pastor Guillermo was thinking, "Well, which is it?" but he knew better than to ask that question out loud!

Your Predecessor

Unless you are organizing a brand-new congregation, you have had a predecessor. And, truth to tell, pastors putting together new faith communities have the predecessors that live in people's memories of other places. Perhaps the pastor before you served this one appointment for fifteen years. Perhaps the pastor before you left after six months with a cloud of suspicion overhead. In either case—or with something in between—you will hear from those who loved . . . disliked . . . trusted . . . supported . . . ignored . . . tolerated your predecessor.

Why do some persons feel it is important to tell you what they thought of your predecessor? It might be a testing of your own views. ("He wanted us to take down the American flag in the sanctuary." The unasked question is "How do you feel about that?") It might be letting you know what this member thinks is a priority for your ministry. ("I love the fact that she insisted we pay our apportionments because that was so much of our mission outreach." The unstated view is "I support everything we do to participate in connectional missions.") It might be simply getting something off the chest. ("I never liked the way some folks treated Brother Hamline. I didn't much care for his way of not visiting, but he was still our pastor.") It might be a helpful clarification of local church division. ("You know, when the charge conference voted not to build a new building—let's see, that was almost twenty years ago—the vote was ten for and eleven against. That created some real conflict in the church, and it still exists in subtle ways. I don't think Pastor Thompson ever quite understood those hidden tensions.") It might be an effort to recruit you for an ongoing church struggle. ("Some people think we ought to stop having that chicken stew fund-raiser we have been having each spring for at least thirty years. Our last pastor insisted we do it. What do you think?") There is a lot going on when church members talk about your predecessor. For one thing, you may well be getting only one part of the story. For another thing, getting identified immediately as pro or con on a divisive issue hinders your ability to lead to a reconciled decision. And, at its most serious level, a pastor can be charged with having "relationships and/or behavior that undermines the ministry of another pastor" (¶ 2702.1[f]). That violation has the potential of severe consequences (¶ 362).

What is a good response when the conversation veers toward your predecessor? "I hear that" or "That must be very important to you" or "The days ahead are going to be interesting, aren't they?" or "I look forward to our ministry together" or "You must be an idiot to talk like that"—uh, maybe not that last one. And, oh, by the way, once you leave this appointment, some folks are going to be talking about you too!

 Here's an idea: As you pray during the early days in the new appointment, put your predecessor on your prayer list.

Prayer: Come, Holy Spirit, bring your fresh power into this place. Amen.

"How do you know so much about your community? You moved the same time I did, but I still get lost getting around and you seem to know all the back roads!" Louise Proctor and Terry Franklin were comparing notes after the short time in their new appointments. Terry replied, "I got some common-sense ideas from a book I read. I'll loan you my copy."

Your Community

Congratulations, dear reader. This is the very book to which Terry Franklin referred! The other day I was about thirty miles from home. I had completed my errand a little quicker than I had anticipated, so I said to myself, "Self, why don't you try something different?" Instead of driving back home the same way I had arrived, I headed out on another road. When I came to an interesting side road, I turned right and followed it. When I came to a stop sign, I decided to turn left. This led me through the small downtown area of a nearby town. Then, I came to an intersection with a major highway. Rather than taking the main route, I crossed over and continued into a quiet rural area. This rolling road passed a megachurch I had never seen. It carried me by a multi-acre family farm that had been turned into an amusement park; I had not even known it existed. All of a sudden I saw a street sign; I was less than a mile from the home of some longtime friends. I made the turn and a few minutes later I was knocking on their door.

I won't bore you with the rest of my drive home, but suffice it to say that by adding a few minutes to my trip, I encountered some beautiful new territory, observed a few areas to avoid at night, got to visit Bill and Glenda, and identified a couple of places to which I would want to return. As I made this trip, my turns and street selections were almost random. I made my way home, but my journey was rich, not routine.

No matter whether your appointment is in a metropolitan area or sixteen miles from the nearest stoplight or where distance is measured in hours, not minutes, try getting lost in your parish! You might stumble across a neighboring United Methodist congregation. You might spot a school with whom your congregation could partner. You might encounter a locale that seems to beg for mission outreach. You might get a broader sense of the demographics of the region. You might come across the store that carries the hard-to-find chocolate candy you love. You might see a park that invites you to bring the family for a picnic. You might even find a shortcut between two places you need to be. And, of course, it might be a waste of time, but I think it is worth the risk.

Here is a variation on that theme of getting lost on purpose. Identify someone in the congregation(s) who knows the community well. Ask him or her to ride with you so you will have a guided tour as you drive about. You might learn some things about the region that would not be obvious to a passing observer. Of course, you will be seeing the community through the lens of your helper. If your members are scattered, ask someone who knows the area to ride with you and point out where various folks live. To avoid misperceptions, consider whether it might be wise to have two people—not just one—join you on these expeditions.

 Here's an idea: Have your GPS at the ready in case you get lost while getting lost!

Prayer: Merciful God, open my eyes that I might glimpse my new community through your eyes of grace and hope. Amen.

The First Month

Tito Perez laughed as he compared "first month notes" with his local pastor mentor (¶ 316.4). Erika Swanson smiled and said, "Don't worry! I have two graduate degrees, have served four different appointments, and I even wrote an article on local church ministry—and I still get surprised! The unexpected just simply goes with the territory!"

Unwanted Gifts

Unexpected? For example, what do you do if someone gives an odd, unwanted gift to the church? I am imagining that one Sunday you step into the worship space and there is something new: a large plastic statue of Elvis kneeling in prayer. "When Aunt Debra died, I knew she would want the church to have this prayer figure that had meant so much to her." Of course, you express appreciation for the generosity of Aunt Debra's nephew. Then, suggest that the church council will explore ideas for the best place to display this objet d'art. (This plants the seed that others will be in on the decision about the statue and that decision might well be not to keep it in the sanctuary.) Keep in mind that the trustees, following the direction of the charge conference, have the authority regarding "acceptance or rejection" of gifts to the church (¶ 2529.3). It certainly is a good idea to have some guidelines in place before walking in on that statue on some glad Sunday morning. Why not have a committee make recommendations to the charge conference (¶¶ 246–47) as to how gifts will be handled? The very nature of unexpected gifts is that they are unexpected, so having a policy in place will protect the role and interests of everyone. One congregation had to decide whether to accept a large financial gift from someone who had won the state-sponsored lottery. "In light of

¶ 163.G (United Methodist opposition to the lottery), how can we in good conscience take this money?" How would you like to have been the pastor when that issue emerged?

Unavailable for Pastoral Care

Unexpected? For example, what do you do if three teenagers from your congregation are involved in an automobile accident and have been rushed to the hospital? Ordinarily, you would drop everything and head to the ER. Ordinarily, you would make sure the parents or guardians had transportation to check on the youth. Ordinarily, you would make a call to start the congregational prayer chain. Ordinarily . . . but you are not in an ordinary circumstance. You might be out-of-town. You might be wiped out by the latest thrust of the flu bug. You might be stranded at home without wheels, because your spouse is out on a fishing expedition. Common sense will give you some alternatives (phone calls, members with cars, public transportation, simply waiting). Often, in addition, pastors have a Plan B, those strategies appropriate or not depending on why you are out-of-pocket. Do you have a clergy colleague who could get to the hospital in your stead? Can you reach the chaplain at the medical center? Have you helped equip key lay personnel to step forward in these caring ministries? (If you inherited persons who are Stephen Ministers (stephen-ministries.org), their gifts might be helpful in this emergency.) Can you have an understanding with a neighbor that you can use his truck without notice, including having your own key? Can you e-mail or text a prayer to the parents? Do you have an e-mail contact list for church members, so they can stay informed and supportive? If you have just arrived at your appointment, there is a good chance some of these responses will not yet be in place, but it just might be that this crisis might also be a gift that energizes such plans for responding.

Calling for Help When Threatened

Unexpected? For example, suppose you are threatened by an intruder or accosted by a thief who has broken into the church and is about to steal the golden candlesticks. Suppose you are helping some stranger who decides that your wallet has some lovely pictures of US luminaries printed on paper. Suppose you are uncertain as to the intent of someone who knocked on your study door. Do you have access to 911? Do you value your life and well-being more than the property you are protecting? There is tension in the risk of helping. Perhaps the hardest questions might be "What is helpful for this person who is confronting me? How do I show God's love?" One thing that will be helpful for both you and your visitor will be as much calmness as you can express.

Once I came upon a man who was stealing clothes from our church clothing closet. When I encountered him in a hallway, I simply said, "Can we pray before you leave?" He stayed. We prayed. He dropped the stack of clothes onto the floor. Then, we talked about ways the church might help.

If you feel uncertainty or menace or simply want to alert someone else of the situation, try using a code word or phrase that will signal your contact that you need help, while not, at the same time, escalating the encounter into rashness. If there is someone else in the building (a custodian, a musician, a secretary) who just happens by or if you have some way to communicate your need, simply use that word or phrase. It will mean nothing to your would-be combatant, but it lets your colleague know of your distress. (I sat across the desk from a man who implied he had a pistol—I never saw it—and he spoke of his anger with churches who didn't care for the needy. I told him that I agreed and said, "Hang on a moment and let me make a change for Sunday's bulletin and then we can talk some more. I called out to the woman who was typing up the bulletin in the next room. "Edna, change the opening hymn to number 64." Edna knew that "64" was our code word at Trinity for "I need some help." As I continued to talk with the man, I heard others outside the door. Happy ending: I breathed a sigh of relief, and another man from the church and I drove the visitor to a nearby homeless shelter.) If this system is to work, key individuals need to know the code. If I had called home and told my son that I heard he had made only a 64 on his exam, he would know that was my call for help. It does not always work, but it is a good plan for backup.

Here's an idea: Make peace with the fact that no matter how carefully you plan, your ministry will sometimes gravitate toward the unexpected.

Prayer: Surprising God, thank you for your presence through curves, detours, dead ends, and straightaways. Amen.

Repton Hall called his predecessor at St. Timothy United Methodist Church. He asked a question and then listened for a moment and said, "I certainly understand and I appreciate your spirit. The Manning family wanted me to ask you, but I'm sure they will understand." Pastor Hall disconnected his phone and said to his wife, "Mr. Blackwell said he never goes back to former appointments for funerals. He said it was not fair to my chance to be a pastor to the Mannings. He also said that from a selfish view he knew that if he did it for one he would have to do it for all. I guess I best get started. I'm nervous already."

Deaths and Funerals

There are so many things that can go wrong at a funeral, and there are so many things that can go right. It is no wonder that Repton Hall was nervous as he began preparing for his first funeral as pastor in charge. It is not surprising that when clergy get together to exchange "how are things going" stories, they often end up saying, "You won't believe what happened at this funeral the other day."

Your pastoral visits after learning of the death can help both you and the family move toward some peace in the midst of loss. These conversations will be filled with memories. As soon as you get back to your car, jot down some highlights of that sharing. Those notes could help you find appropriate ways to personalize the "naming" portion of the Service of Death and Resurrection (see no. 870 in *The United Methodist Hymnal*).

Although some families will have done some advance thought about a funeral or memorial service—and a few persons will have left directives or suggestions—it is much more common for the pastor to have to lead the family in making such decisions. After the death of a loved one (or a not-so-loved-one), the survivors may find their tensions and differences in full blossom. "Papa would want chrysanthemums and sunflowers next to his casket; those were his favorites." "Why are you insisting on those flowers? You know they make me sneeze." "This isn't about you; it is about Papa." "No, it's not about Papa; it is about you trying to have your own way." You, as the pastor, will have to decide: Is that conflict the "elephant in the room" or are the unmade plans for the service the "elephant in the room"?

I recall how I failed to be helpful in my first such visit. In an effort to be supportive and healing, I began offering comforting words and assurances from Scripture. The wife of the deceased continued to be nervous and obviously ill at ease, so I kicked my reassurances up a notch. It did not help. The discomfort in the room was palpable. Finally, the widow took matters into her own hands: "Reverend, I know all that. What I want to know is what are we going to do about the funeral?"

She was right. There are practical matters to be determined. Public service or private service? Where will it be? When will it be? Will there be a special time for friends and family to gather (sometimes called a wake or a visitation or a viewing)? Which funeral home is helping? What will the service be like? Music? Scripture? Speakers? Pallbearers? Burial? Cremation? What about the cemetery? What about cultural traditions?

You are not empty-handed as you make these designs with the family. Good starting places are "A Service of Death and Resurrection" in *The United Methodist Hymnal* (nos. 870–75) and "Services of Death and Resurrection" in *The United Methodist Book of Worship* (139–71). The latter has suggestions for services, including, among others, one that includes Holy Communion, one for persons who are not in the Christian faith community, and one for a stillborn child. There are helps for the family hour or wake (or visitation), and prayers for a variety of settings related to death. *The Book of Worship* is going to be your friend!

Here are some issues you might face.

Rites of a Fraternal Order

What if the family wants part of the service to be with traditions from a fraternal order? (On one web search, I found over eighty such organizations, some for men, some for women, and some for both.) As pastor, you are responsible for seeing that the worship experience is not compromised. If the organization's rites seem intrusive or inappropriate, could they be offered at a separate time? An alternative is to invite the special tradition to precede the service of death and resurrection. If the ritual is to be used at the graveside, some pastors complete the service of committal (*The United Methodist Book of Worship* 155–57) and then step aside for a closure by the fraternal order. Other clergy determine that the last word at the grave should be the pastoral benediction. Almost all fraternal organizations seek to cooperate with the pastor and recognize that the pastor's choices (in conjunction with the family) are to be accepted. Unless there are the gravest of abuses of Scripture and Wesleyan theology, these pastoral connections in the midst of the sorting out of emotions and relief and sadness are not the occasions for insisting on pastoral self-indulgence of theological subtlety. There are, of course, times for teaching, but most people will not be ready to learn while they are reeling with the aftershock of death.

Military Honors

What are possibilities if the family wants recognition of the military life of the deceased? In some settings, the widow/widower/son/daughter/partner/friend/kinfolk may simply want the coffin to be draped with their nation's flag. In other settings, arrangements will have been made for a military honor guard, perhaps forming two rows of personnel so the coffin is carried in a recessional between the two. Perhaps, there will be a bugler who will play "Taps" as the graveside ceremony is completed. (It is said that Winston Churchill requested that taps be played at his funeral, to be followed by reveille, the military signal for the start of a new day.) There may be a three-volley salute from a nearby rifle. (This custom began centuries ago in Europe when battles were halted so the dead and wounded could be removed from the battlefield; the three rifle shots signaled that the battle could continue.) If the flag has been placed over the coffin, military personnel may carefully and with great dignity remove the flag, fold it crisply, and then present it to one of the survivors of their military colleague. (I was one of the pastors presiding at one such graveside service. The deceased had remarried after the death of his wife; his children, themselves adults, detested their father's new wife and said that they would grab the flag away from this woman if the soldier handed it to her instead of to one of them. I was glad that my colleague pastor was the one who would be close enough to respond if a fracas interrupted the poignant moment! I watched as the uniformed man hesitated for just a moment and then he presented the flag, with the traditional words expressing the nation's gratitude, to the eager daughter. Then, I breathed again.) The military recognition honors one aspect of the life of the deceased; its sheer drama may dominate the imagery of the day. The gospel's long-sustaining power is what you can offer the bereaved.

Open Casket

What do you do for a funeral if no one has died? OK. That is a trick question. According to my local paper, no one died in our entire county in the past couple of days. Two people "passed away." One person "went home to Jesus." Another individual "woke up in heaven." But no one *died*. Death is often such a brazen invader into our lives that we slip into various modes of denial. Perhaps the softer language helps us deal with the harshness of loss and the depth of hurt, but the reality is "Katherine Watson is dead." For some persons, seeing the dead body in a casket is the strongest shattering of illusion. Even the most gifted cosmetic work by the morticians cannot deny the truth of death. Acknowledging the actuality of death is a healthy way to move toward healing. This leads some families to wonder: Should the coffin be open during the funeral service? *The United Methodist Book of Worship* "presupposes that the encounter with the body of the deceased and the closing of the coffin have already taken place, and for this reason the coffin remains closed throughout the service and thereafter" (140 [5]). The closed casket allows worshipers (including immediate mourners) to focus on the gospel's triumphant encounter with death.

Your Own Grieving

How do you handle your own grief and mourning? I hope it is not callous to say that sometimes conducting a funeral can be likened to just another day at the office. There are times, however, when you are as deeply captured by a death as anyone else. A longtime friend. A trusted colleague. A congregational matriarch. A family member. A sudden tragedy. I conducted the funeral for my aunt and later for my uncle, but I chose not to have a leadership role at my mother's service. I gave a eulogy (sometimes called "naming" or "witness") at the memorial service for my friend-since-childhood, but I did not speak at my wife's funeral. You will know when you cannot be the non-anxious presence that the pastoral role needs. Of course, there is nothing wrong in sharing in your congregation's sorrow, but be aware that your own broken spirit may not give the gathered community the entrance it needs into healing. You certainly need the space to be human and to do your own journey of woe, but presiding at a service of worship such as a funeral is seldom the best setting for that. Maybe it will help to take a few days away from church activities. Maybe there is a neighboring pastor who can hear your story. Maybe you can develop new intentionality about your own devotional habits. Some annual conferences have counselors whose professional responsibility is with clergy. One resource you might use is *Healing After Loss: Daily Meditations for Working Through Grief* by Martha Whitmore Hickman (New York: William Morrow, 1994). Even our Lord found a time and place for such weeping (John 11:35, Luke 19:41). It's OK to have a good cry.

Unknown Deceased

How do you plan a funeral for someone no one seems to know? It might not happen this week or next week, but at some point in your ministry, you will probably be called upon to conduct a burial for someone whom no one seems to remember. There is no family from whom to gather stories. There is no awareness by members of the congregation as to who this person was. There is no way to connect with this individual's journey. Perhaps, the funeral home has called and told you that they have the body of a homeless man who was delivered to their door. Perhaps some unidentified person was driving down the nearby interstate and was killed in a car accident. Perhaps a mortuary employee says that among the papers found in the hospital room of the deceased was a request to be buried by a United Methodist pastor. You may know the name. You may not even know the name. In such cases as these, it is likely that only you and the funeral home personnel will be in attendance at the grave. To me, that didn't feel right, so I have invited the lay leader or others from the congregation to join me for the ritual. I have used much of the ritual from "A Service of Committal" (*The United Methodist Book of Worship* 155–57), keeping in mind that I actually do not know anything about the faith journey of the deceased.

A homily raises the questions: What can we say about someone that none of us know? What can we say about every child of God? What can we say that is universally true? It is a time to make claim upon the assertion that all of us are created in the image of God (Genesis 1:26). It is a time to recall that all things, including humankind, have been created by and for Christ (Colossians 1:16). It is time to acknowledge that there has never been a time in this person's life that God did not care (Isaiah 46:3-4). It is time to remember that there is much about each of us that others do not know but God does (Jeremiah 23:24). It is a time to admit that we do not need to know a person's story to know that he or she has sinned (Romans 3:23). It is time to celebrate that God's love is not defined by our worthiness (Romans 5:8). Here is much that can be said about this one known only to God! Are there loved ones somewhere who do not know what has happened to this one? Pray for them. Are there individuals who have been harmed in some way by this child of God? Pray for them. Are there women and men who are better off because of some kindness done by this person? Pray for them. And, finally, we commit this one into God's mercy and care.

Here's an idea: Keep a record of the death date of persons for whom you conduct a service; on the anniversary of that date, send a note to let the survivors know of your continued prayerful support.

Prayer: God of all eternity, help me in my frailty as I move as
your servant in times and places of death. Amen.

———————

Jacob Lightfoot looked again at the e-mail from his district superintendent. "Remember that the deadline for filing Table I, Table II, and Table III is only a week away. I want our district to be 100 percent in getting these in on time. It is an important part of our accountability in the United Methodist connection." Pastor Lightfoot studied the report forms once more. He thought to himself, *I wonder what this has to do with ministry. Why does the D.S. think this is so all-fired important?*

Personal Records

Some people love to keep records. They set up Excel spreadsheets for everything from recording weight gain and loss to noting how many pages have been read in a day. Other people, not so much. For them, it is burdensome to have to fill out name and amount on an offering envelope. Both of these kinds of people are called by God for ministry.

Accounts of your ministry are best kept as things happen. It is not easy to try to remember, three months later, the full name of the baby you baptized. Was it Edgar Percy Phillips or was it Percy Edgar Phillips or was it "Smiley," which is what everybody seems to call him now? Sermons preached. Weddings conducted. Funerals led. Baptisms celebrated. Members received. Buildings consecrated. Salaries received. Some of these things need to be noted for your personal memory; some are called for as official church records (¶ 230, for example).

How do you go about maintaining some sense of order for these registers? Let's think first about the pastoral information that is for your own personal archives and ruminations. (Later we'll look at developing the records for reports to be made to the charge conference or to the annual conference.)

How OCD are you about keeping score? In one of my appointments, I developed a system of keeping track of my pastoral visits: hospital, home, work, newcomers, and so on. I did it on index cards; these days I'd probably put it into a computer file. Each time I visited someone, I made an index card with the name on the top, followed by the date. If I visited that person a second time, I'd pull that card and add the new date. This gave me an alphabetical record of these pastoral contacts. It helped me see if there were gaps in my being in touch with some families. It gave me information for a family member who said "Aunt Maude says you never come to see her when she is sick." It turned out that Aunt Maude was slipping a bit in the memory department, and I was able to let the family know how I had tried to stay in touch with her.

A tool that will not likely be very interesting for a few years, but which will be a gold mine in years to come, is a record of sermons delivered. This could be as simple as starting a computer file to which you add, week-by-week, the date, title (if you have one), text, place sermon was given, and any special remarks, for each sermon. Here is a place you could note if Communion was served. Here you have notice of times you preached in places other than your own appointment. After you have been at this for ten years or so, you might not recall just how many times you preached at St. Swithens-by-the-Swamp or what your sermon was on your first Sunday as pastor at Mount Saint Gooseberry United Methodist Church. (For better or worse—I still don't know if this was a good idea—at one appointment where I served for seven years, I preached the exact same sermon on my first and my last Sundays in that pulpit. Yes, I told the congregation what I was doing. My sermons are not usually something folks remember seven years later!) If you are not using the lectionary, this list will be a good place to double-check any propensity to keep drawing water from the exact same biblical well.

Another good record to keep is a listing of all persons you have baptized. It is helpful to make note of the date, the full name of the person baptized, and, in the case of a child, the name of the parents. You could also include the age of the person baptized and where the baptism took place. If local church records are not maintained accurately, your personal account may be helpful to someone who needs to prove his or her age for some purpose such as eligibility for Social Security. Some pastors send an annual note to children, reminding them of the day they were baptized. For someone who was baptized as an infant, this stirs the truth that "God loved me before I knew it."

I started keeping my own list of persons received into church membership at places I served. At first, I listed only date, name, and congregation. Later, I decided to make note of whether the new member made a profession of faith (¶ 217), transferred from another United Methodist church (¶ 229, ¶ 239), came from another denomination (¶ 225), or was an affiliate or associate member (¶ 227). One time after I started keeping the list with these designations, my ego took a hit. I was curious to see how many persons had made professions of faith under my ministry. Because I had not used that "profession of faith" identifier in my earlier record keeping, I wrote back to one of my successor pastors and asked him to check the official congregation records to see which of the persons I received into membership had made a profession of faith. Ah, the burst of pride I felt when he answered "seventeen!" And he told me which ones. Then, alas, he gave me the rest of the story: "Only two of these are still active in the church." Ouch! (There are other membership situations too numerous to mention; look at the category "membership" under "local church" in the index in *The Book of Discipline*.)

Looking back over the pages of weddings at which I presided, I see all sorts of interesting things. I remember the one that was subdued because it was the same day as President Kennedy was assassinated. I see that the youngest bride was fifteen years old; the oldest groom was eighty. For each ceremony, I give the date, the full names of the couple, their ages, and where the ritual took place. Marriages create legal relationships; keeping tabs on the weddings at which you "signed the papers" will give you and others another layer of evidence if the legality of the marriage is called into question. Later in this volume, we'll talk about the actual wedding ceremony and the pastoral work that leads up to it.

What information might you keep about funerals that you conduct? I write down the date of the funeral or memorial service; you might like also to include the date of death. In addition to the name of the deceased, type in his or her age. (There is a dose of reality when you observe that the one who has died is the same age as you are.) If you do a homily, you can make a memo as to the text and/or title. Where did the service take place? Where did the burial take place? This is another collection of data that will not mean much to you in the beginning years of your ministry, but in the reflective years to come, you will be blessed to have these tools for jogging your memory and underscoring just how precious and sacred these pastoral responsibilities can be.

There are, of course, any number of records you can keep. How about a list of your appointments? How about a notation as to membership numbers (or some other statistic) when you came and when you left? You can trace how your compensation changed over the years. Make a column for the times you preached in some setting other than your own appointment. Have you engaged in a major fund-raising effort? Perhaps there is a space to delineate important dates in your ministry journey: candidacy, education, licensing, appointment, and so on. (I've also included in my notable events category the dates of significant family events, as well as unusual congregational activities—unveiling a historical marker, burying a time capsule, first service in new building, service of dedication when a building debt is paid.)

If you like to create your own electronic files, go for it! You might find some helps by doing a web search for electronic pastoral records. If you prefer to keep written records, Abingdon Press publishes the book *Pastoral Record*.

 Here's an idea: Start a written or electronic record of your ministry from the very beginning.

Prayer: Holy Spirit, you are planting the seeds of memory in my life even now. Wash over me with the joys and hopes of my tomorrows. Amen.

Jacob Lightfoot put down his cell phone. His colleague, an experienced pastor down the road at Main Street United Methodist Church, had agreed to meet with him to go over the required reports in Table I, Table II, Table III. Even with the help promised, Pastor Lightfoot called out to his wife, "I may be gone for a while. George said it would take some time to go through these report tables." He jumped into his car and went off to meet George Baker.

Reports

Back in the day—early 1900s—rather than submitting written reports, each pastor gave an oral accounting of ministry at our annual conference. Legend has it that at one such session, the bishop called on the pastor from the Pasquotank Circuit to give his report. The members of the annual conference quietly groaned because this four-point charge had the reputation of being one of the most dreary places for ministry; year after year its pastor would state that there had been no professions of faith, that the finances were in disarray, and that attendance was drifting toward single digits. But this time, the pastor began his statement, "Bishop, on the Pasquotank Circuit, things are looking up." The annual conference perked up, alert now to hear the good news from this usually drab setting. "Bishop," he began, "on the Pasquotank Circuit things are looking up. It's the only way you can see when you are flat on your back."

From the days of the Wesleys' "Holy Club" at Oxford University and Philip William Otterbein's self-imposed discipline and Jacob Albright's sacrificial participation in small group accountability, the strands that form The United Methodist Church have expected members to report on "How is it with your soul?" and "What is the fruit of your ministry?" and "Who is in your fellowship?" These days, the questions are worded differently, but we still answer to one another about the joys and disappointments that make up our life together. Is it too much to find some parallel in the theological language that notes that sanctification is a gift that follows justification?

United Methodists recognize that we are in this together (a connectional people) so that both the aforementioned Pasquotank Circuit and the high-steepled church on Main Street are responsible to one another. That is how we are expressing our responsibility to God. The full story cannot be told in numbers, but such statistics open the door for the conversation. It's like temperature and blood pressure checks at your medical exam. Those figures do not tell everything about your health, but they certainly offer a clue. Do you hesitate to go to the doctor because you have not taken care of your health? Do you resist going to the annual physical because you know that some of your bad condition is your fault? Do you dread what the doctor might say even though you have worked as hard as you can to do the healthy things? Do you simply not want to find out if the news is bad? These same rationales may depict why some clergy resist the effort and energy it takes to make reports. Lack of accountability? Concern that numbers don't give the true picture? Feeling that time could be better spent? Dread of the inevitable? All of the above?

But it is not just hard-headed pencil pushers (Does anybody really push a pencil anymore?) that call us clergy to complete these forms. How about Isaiah 30:8? ("Go now, write it before them on a tablet, and inscribe it in a book, so that it may be for the time to come as a witness forever.") How about Romans 14:12? ("So then, each of us will be accountable to God.") What about Judges 6:13b? ("And where are all his wonderful deeds that our ancestors recounted to us?")

In addition to whatever personal records you keep for yourself, you will be expected to file a pastor's report to the charge conference (including ¶¶ 231, 232, 247.15, in addition to any requirements by the annual conference). Others will also be making reports to the charge conference. We shall explore those records a few pages over. The other major statistical accounting is the annual completion of Table I, Table II, and Table III. Unless otherwise instructed, you make these reports for the calendar year, January 1–December 31. The General Council on Finance and Administration (a denomination-wide group) is authorized to establish these reporting systems (¶¶ 807.15, 807.16). Yesterday was the best time to make sure you are going to be able to gather the information you need for those reports. If you didn't do it yesterday, do it today! That's why this section comes early in the book.

There are three good companions for your work on these accounts of ministry. (1) Go to your conference website and track down the name of the conference statistician. This is the person for your FAQs—frequently asked questions—and, in many conferences, the one to whom the reports are sent. (2) Good ol' George at the next United Methodist church down the road has done these tables for twenty years. I bet George can help. (3) Go to the website of the General Council on Finance and Administration (gcfa.org) and choose the link called "General Church Resources" that takes you to a page called "Forms and Resources." Scroll down to the heading titled "Statistical Reports" and find beneath it Table I, Table II, and Table III.

Of course, when in doubt, get in touch with the district superintendent.

How you complete and file these statistical records varies from annual conference to annual conference. In some conferences, this work is done entirely with electronic forms. In other annual conferences, you will be asked to send a hard copy to a designated office. There are conferences who ask each pastor to come in person to bring his or her Tables I–II–III to a specified collector.

The information requested will basically be the same for all pastors, but, from time to time, an annual conference might choose its own vocabulary to title a question or might even add inquiry about some matters of particular interest in that annual conference's life. This can change labels from one conference to the next and can alter the way the tallies are numbered. For the purposes of these descriptions, I shall use the terms and numbering employed on the website of the General Council on Finance and Administration. (Remember your friend gcfa.org? You can send questions to them at gcfa@gcfa.org.)

If you are serving a multi-point charge, you need to complete these tables separately for each congregation.

There are three categories of items to be reported: Table I is about "Membership and Participation." Table II is about "Church Assets and Expenses." Table III is about "Church Income." Take a deep breath and then let's look at each requested datum.

Table I

Table I pertains to "Membership and Participation." (If you are pastor of a federated church or yoked parish [¶208], report only that part of the membership with membership in The United Methodist Church. Don't worry; if these terms do not make sense to you, it almost certainly means you are not "federated" or "yoked!")

1. Total professing members reported at the close of last year. For this information, you are dependent upon the report filed by the pastor last year. It will likely be item 9 in last year's Table I: Total professing members reported at the close of this year. You can find last year's Table in your *Conference Journal* (either printed or online). If you cannot locate it, contact your new friend, the conference statistician. You might also look in the third drawer from the top in the second filing cabinet on the right in the back closet of the church fellowship hall. What if it is obvious that your predecessor lied through the teeth in reporting this number—I mean, what if it is obvious that your predecessor had a grand vision of growth? The GCFA (General Council on Finance and Administration) form provides columns for noting any corrections—items 2d and 3c. Occasionally, a conference will have "A Year of Jubilee" (Leviticus 25:8-15) in which all errors are forgiven and can be corrected without any imputed wrong. If you are not sure, contact your new BFF, the conference statistician, or your kind district superintendent.

2a. Received this year by Profession of Faith through confirmation.

2b. Received this year by Profession of Faith other than through confirmation. These two items (2a and 2b) state how many persons made first-time professions of Christian faith in the past calendar year. (There is another place to indicate how many are restored after a lapse in membership.) The official congregational record is the one kept by the membership secretary (¶¶ 230, 233, 234). Early in your time as pastor at a congregation, find out who the membership secretary is and make sure that both of you have the same understanding of this recordkeeping. You will need to work as a team to keep these rolls accurate and up-to-date (¶ 235). In this Table I accounting, you only give a number; in your report to the charge conference, you will give names. (Paragraph 233 describes the electronic or print-based permanent church records for this membership information.) Although it is seldom activated, there is a provision for the annual conference to make inquiry about a local church where no members have been received on confession of faith (¶ 604.9).

2c. Membership restored by Affirmation of Faith. This will probably be an unusual listing. If there is someone who made a previous profession of faith but who later withdrew from membership, he or she could be restored to membership by an affirmation of that previous profession (¶¶ 230.1[f], 242). This would also apply to someone returned to membership after having been removed from membership by charge conference action (¶¶ 228.2b[4], 242).

2d. Added by Correction. Here is where you would correct a previous year's error if that correction would add members to the membership record. For example, suppose that last year the membership secretary was absent on the Sunday two persons transferred membership to the church and did not know about the action. Your predecessor was more careless about these things than you are, so that colleague failed to mention it to the membership secretary. It never got into the books. Last year's number would have been off by two. Here is where you would add those two.

2e. Transferred in from another United Methodist Church. There are provisions for persons moving membership from one United Methodist congregation to another (¶ 239). The number will be the total account of persons who joined your congregation by such a transfer.

2f. Transferred in from a non-United Methodist Church. Did persons join your congregation from a church in another denomination? Did someone become a member of your church by transferring from a nondenominational fellowship? Even if the "sending church" does not issue any kind of certificate of transfer, you would still include those transfers in this column (¶ 225). Note that *The Book of Discipline* speaks of baptism as being "administered in the name of the triune God." Consequently, if someone wished to transfer membership from a tradition that did not practice triune baptism (for example, The Church of Jesus Christ of Latter-day Saints), that person would need to be baptized in the name of the triune God before becoming a United Methodist.

3a. Removed by Charge Conference Action. Paragraph 228.2b contains some of the saddest portions of *The Book of Discipline*. Here are noted several ways in which a person might involuntarily or under difficult circumstances be removed from church membership. Have they simply been negligent of membership vows (¶ 228.2b[1][4])? Has their relocation meant they no longer participate in church life (¶ 228.2b[2][4])? Have they moved and no one knows how to reach them (¶ 228.2b[3][4])? Prayerful integrity may lead the charge conference to take action to remove these names from membership. Some churches refer to this process as "cleaning the rolls," but it also means some rupture in the care of members.

3b. Withdrawn from Professing Membership. Someone may simply decide to forgo church membership and voluntarily withdraw from that relationship (¶ 230.1e). Perhaps someone simply joins another denomination without any notice to the United Methodist congregation (¶ 241). Has there been a written complaint or grievance filed against the member, resulting in either voluntary (¶ 228.2b[9]) or involuntary (¶ 2714.6) termination of membership? In every one of these cases, there is the pain of brokenness in the body of Christ.

3c. Removed by Correction. There is a classic story of a pastor who went through the church cemetery each year when it was time to complete Table I. He dutifully jotted down a few names of the deceased to add to the roll, saying, "They are doing the church as much good now as they did when they were alive." Hmmm. You may inherit an incorrect number from last year's report. Instead of the 107 members shown on the membership secretary's records, there is a generous tally of 117 members. Typo? Maybe. Error in tabulating? Maybe. Deliberate inflation? No comment. This correction will be an opportunity to set right that figure by subtracting the extra.

3d. Transferred out to another United Methodist Church. This is fairly straightforward as you check the record for the number of folks who took their membership from your church and had it moved to another United Methodist congregation. (Look at ¶ 239; there are recommended certificates to use.) Sometimes it is obvious why Bertha Braxton had her membership transferred to a church in her new home out-of-state in Ohio. It might not be as clear as to why Edgar Howington wanted to join another United Methodist congregation around the corner from yours. There may be pastoral reflections and self-examination that go along with tabulating this number.

3e. Transferred out to a non-United Methodist Church. Are they upset with the denomination? Is there no United Methodist church near where they have moved? Do they want to get back to the denomination of their roots? Have they had a theological struggle with Wesleyan thought? Do they feel United Methodism has deserted key principles of one of its predecessor denominations? Is there an attraction to a congregation that better fits their family profile? Most of the time it will be clear why someone has left The United Methodist Church. The question for you is "Should this be a matter of pastoral concern?" (Review ¶ 240; there is an official form that is to be used.)

3f. Deceased. This number, of course, is not an accounting of how many funerals you personally have conducted during the past year; it is reference to the number of members who died, regardless of where a service was held, by whom, or even if a service was not held (¶ 235). There are times that the death of an out-of-town member is not discovered until years after the fact. It is appropriate to include that death in the figures for the year on which you are working, even though the death occurred some years earlier. After all, the report is of when the name was removed from the membership roll, not when the death happened.

4. Total Professing Members at the close of this year. Here is where you do all the adding and subtracting of the numbers in items 2 through 3. Note that this number is of *professing* members (¶ 217). It does not include affiliate or associate members (¶ 227) and does not include baptized members who have not yet become professing members (¶ 215). Confusion can occur because the term *membership* is used both for persons who have been baptized but who have not made a profession of faith (¶ 215.1) and for baptized persons who come into membership by profession of faith (¶ 215.2). Note the language of ¶ 215.3 of *The Book of Discipline*: "For statistical purposes, church membership is equated to the number of people listed on the roll of professing members." That is what is being reported in Table I, Item 4. (Baptized members, as well as professing members, are considered members of the local church, members of the worldwide United Methodist connection, and members of the church universal (¶ 215.4).) This may be a case in which theological language/insight and common vocabulary have not kept pace with one another. There is a place later in Table I where the number of *baptized* *members* is noted. This current item 4, however, is where *professing members* are counted.

The next range of inquiries may be considered offensive by some. You are asked to identify your professing members by racial/ethnic categories and by gender identity. Because of St. Paul's reminder in Galatians 3:28 ("There is no longer Jew or Greek, there is no longer slave or free, there is no longer male and female; for all of you are one in Christ Jesus."), this way of dividing us up may seem foreign to the gospel. However, it is precisely because of our accountability to this scriptural description that we poll ourselves in this way. How well are we doing in matching this "oneness in Christ"? Who is being left out from the full family Table? Are we so focused on one part of God's people, that there is evidence that others "do not fit"? Does our congregation's profile compare to the parish we serve? Reviewing the answers to these items can be, at minimum, an exploration of conscience.

How do you gather this information? If your predecessors have prepared these tabulations, it is simply a matter of reviewing the list of new members and the list of those no longer members and then making the appropriate additions or subtractions in each category. If these data do not exist or earlier reports seem to have been pious guesses, you might be able to come up with figures after a conversation with your membership secretary or other trusted leaders. In some cases you may not know how a person self-identifies and, failing a one-on-one dialogue, may have to decide how the community regards that individual. Statistical accuracy is, of course, important, but the goal of this report is to allow your congregation to measure itself against the inclusivity claimed by The United Methodist Church. (See ¶ 4 of the Constitution of The United Methodist Church in *The Book of Discipline:* the pivotal language is, "All persons without regard to race, color, national origin, status, or economic condition." The 2016 General Conference proposed a constitutional amendment that would change that language to "race, color, gender, national origin, ability, age, marital status or economic condition." As of this writing, the annual conferences have not voted on that amendment.) The following are the racial/ethnic groups used in these subsets of Item 5. The total of all these groups should equal your answer to Number 4.

5a. Asian. A working definition from the General Council on Finance and Administration (Remember our friend gcfa.org?) says these would be people with origins and/or heritage in any of the indigenous peoples of Asia, Southeast Asia, or the Indian Subcontinent. Examples given include Bangladesh, Cambodia, China, India, Indonesia, Japan, Korea, Laos, Malaysia, Myanmar, Pakistan, Philippines, Singapore, Sri Lanka, Taiwan, Thailand, and Vietnam.

5b. Black. These are professing members with origins and/or heritage in the black African racial groups of Africa, the Caribbean, or North, Central, or South America. The overwhelmingly vast majority of black United Methodists in our worldwide denomination do not live in America. You will, of course, be sensitive to the language people use in their own self-description.

5c. Hispanic/Latino. GCFA suggests that here you count people (regardless of race) who have ethnic origins in Latin America. This includes Mexico, Central America, and the Spanish-speaking islands of the Caribbean. This may be a particularly telling statistic for a congregation that is in a community that is undergoing a shift in racial/ethnic presence.

5d. Native American. Here is another tool offered on the GCFA website: "Members with ethnic origins in indigenous America (including Aleut, Inuit, Micmac, Ojibwa, Mayan, Miskito, etc.) and/or who maintain cultural identification through tribal affiliation or community recognition." Sometimes, these members will classify themselves by a tribal name: Choctaw, Navaho, Cherokee, and so on.

5e. Pacific Islander. Again, the defining term is "origins." Which of your members would so identify with Pacific Islands such as Fiji, Kiribati, Guam, Hawaii, Samoa, or Tonga? This can be complicated. Kiribati itself, for example, has more than thirty islands, of which about two-thirds are populated. With such an array of possibilities, double-check with how members self-identify.

5f. White. Here you would count professing members who have ethnic origins in Europe. In a community where "white" is the norm, persons may not think of themselves in terms of their family roots or their cultural practices. In the United States, this is the predominant category for many congregations, but that would not be true in the rapidly growing annual conferences of Africa and the Philippines. Keep in mind: there is a significant distinction between "dominating" and "largest."

5g. Multiracial. Some members see their origins and/or heritage in two or more of the other listed categories. A few pastors have counted all their members in this list, claiming that if we go back far enough we all have both common and mixed ancestors. "We are all multiracial." Although there is certainly some reality in that perception, lumping everyone into one box does little to help us see the broken places in our hospitality, our witness, and our common life.

5. Total Membership Ethnicity. Per Table I: (5a+5b+5c+5d+5e+5f+5g = 5 = 4) What are the implications for what you have learned in this counting process? Who would have thought that a required annual report might help shape the agenda for those who help strategize about evangelism, mission, education and worship for your congregation!

6a. Female/6b. Male. The total of these lines should equal the number is Item 4 (total professing members at the close of this year). If these figures seem to be on target in the most recent Table I, you can simply add or subtract by analyzing how many men and how many women have become new professing members and how many of each are no longer members. It doesn't take much observation to figure out how someone presents himself or herself to the community as male or female. If you have a member who is in the process of transgendering or who chooses to label self as "binary," prayerful conversation might be helpful. Pastoral support in such a situation is more important than precise numerical reporting. (See ¶ 161 F in *The Book of Discipline*.)

6. Total Membership Gender Per Table I: (6a + 6b = 6 = 4)

As Jacob Lightfoot continued his conversation with George Baker, he laughed and said, "George, confession is good for the soul, so here is the truth: I made a D- in third grade arithmetic! All this adding and subtracting and counting people has my head spinning." George smiled and replied, "If it makes you feel any better, it doesn't get any easier after twenty years in the ministry!" Jacob gave a good-natured groan.

Here's an idea: Find a copy of last year's Table I and go over the reported numbers with your membership secretary. Ask: How can we work together to make sure we have these figures ready when it is time to fill out this form?

Prayer: Savior Jesus, you taught that a good shepherd counts the sheep and knows when one is missing. Help me know who is missing in this place and go with me as I go searching. Amen.

"Now," George said, as he picked up a copy of the most recent *Conference Journal*, "This next item may be the most suspect of all." He paused and looked at Jacob Lightfoot. "Brother, do you know the difference in how ushers count attendance and how pastors count attendance?" Lightfoot shook his head "No." George continued, "Ushers count noses; pastors count nostrils. Maybe that is why pastors don't want their ushers to fill out this form!"

The next report for Table I is "average attendance at all weekly services." Then, there are requests for information about persons baptized, nonmember constituents of the church, confirmation classes, all small group ministries, Sunday church school, United Methodist Men, United Methodist Women, mission projects, and the average shoe-size of all left-handed people in your congregation. (Well, no. It does not go quite that far!) These figures are not all going to be found in any one source. It might be a good plan to alert various folks that you are going to count on their knowing the answer when the time comes to crank out Table I. (This might be a good time to ratchet up your prayer life; we haven't even started looking at Table II and Table III.) Ready?

7. Average attendance at all weekly worship services. Is someone counting attendance each week? Is there an ongoing record of those numbers? Why don't you ask the person(s) assigned to do this to give you a report after each service? That will give you a backup storage system for the information (uh, you are the backup). The figure in Item 7 is the grand total of all regularly held services. Although most of these will be on Sunday, you can include others that are considered primary worship services of the congregation. Yes, this is an average; you count both Easter Sunday and the Sunday after Easter! GCFA advises that you should count all persons (including children) who participate in part of any of these services. Less clear choices might include children and caregivers who are in a supervised nursery during worship, Scout troops from the church who have worship off-site on a camping outing, and persons who watch a live stream of the service or enjoy a radio broadcast. The intent of this average worship attendance calculation is to provide a way to examine year-by-year the worship gatherings of the congregation. For that reason, it is important that the same criteria be used from year to year. Otherwise, comparison will not be very useful. If you discover a gigantic disparity between last year's reported number and what your accounting shows, you might alert your district superintendent as to why there seems to be such a difference. The simplest and best guideline might be: "live bodies in the worship space."

7a. Number of persons who worship online. Per Table I, this is: "Report here average weekly number of unique viewers who access worship online. This includes those live streaming your worship service and views/downloads of recorded worship services (audio or video), sermons, and/or podcasts. Do not include generic hits/visits to your website."

8a. Number of persons baptized this year ages 0–12. This report puts legs on the United Methodist teaching that "The Baptism of young children is to be retained in the Church" (¶ 104, Article XVII of The Articles of Religion of The Methodist Church) and "We believe children are under the atonement of Christ and as heirs of the Kingdom of God are acceptable subjects for Christian Baptism" (¶ 104, Article VI of The Confession of Faith of The Evangelical United Brethren Church). In this regard, take a look at ¶ 226, "Care of Children and Youth." It is your responsibility to see that the membership secretary adds the full name of the baptized child to the membership record (¶ 226.2b.) You do not have to report that the infant cried vociferously and spit up on you during the ritual.

8b. Number of persons baptized this year ages 13 or older. The choice of 13 years as the breakpoint in these reports is an informed, but arbitrary decision. Some children are fully into spiritual accountability at 10 years and others are still not mature in that regard at age 17. Although you may have good personal lists of these baptisms, those data go with you when you move. Make sure that the official ongoing records of the church maintain this information. Paragraph 220 speaks of the ministry that is the responsibility of all baptized persons. Reviewing ¶ 216 will remind you of some of your leadership in this relationship.

8. Total number of persons baptized this year (8a + 8b).

9. Total baptized members who have not become professing members. It might help to go back and look again at the comments made above in relation to Item 4 ("Professing Members"). For Item 9, include anyone (regardless of age) who has been baptized, but who has not taken the vows of professing membership. Often, this is your roll of "baptized members." For statistical purposes, you include here only persons who have never been professing members. So, for example, you would not count someone who has withdrawn from professing membership or who had that membership terminated by charge conference action. They remain baptized members, but are not included in this item that notes only those who have not ever become professing members.

10. Number of other constituents of the church. This is a difficult number to ascertain. Paragraph 230.3 spells out that the Constituency Roll has "the names and addresses of such persons as are not members of the church concerned, including unbaptized children, youth, and adults whose names are not on the membership record, and other nonmembers for whom the local church has pastoral responsibility." This might include someone who only attends the Tuesday afternoon Bible study, but is otherwise unaffiliated with the church. This might include an unbaptized youth who takes part in the United Methodist Youth Fellowship. Does it include the newcomer who is "testing out" your church, but has attended for six months? Does it include someone who is a regular at your food pantry, but who has never worshiped with the congregation? How about an unchurched woman whom you visit regularly at the nursing home? The challenging thing is defining "pastoral responsibility." Maybe you think of those unbaptized and nonmembers who are directly affected by your fulfilling "Responsibilities and Duties of Elders and Licensed Pastors" (¶ 340). The other ingredient to keep in mind is "Do they have a relationship with the congregation?" So, you place on the constituency roll those unbaptized and nonmembers who are served by your ministry and who relate to the congregation.

11a. Number of CHILDREN Christian Formation Groups (CFG) participants and leaders (ages 0–11). The general interpretation of the term *children* refers to those who are ages 0 to 11. Some of these children may be in church-sponsored scouting programs (or other such agencies); those numbers would be included only if the program is "wholly integrated with the church's education ministry." (That's a GCFA definition.) Remember: children are counted only once even if they are involved in more than one Christian formation ministry. Paragraph 256.2 will give you a boost in thinking about settings for children's spiritual growth.

11b. Number of YOUTH CFG participants and leaders (ages 12–18). For the purposes of this report, generally use the age range of 12 to 18. (Interestingly, *The Book of Discipline*—¶ 256.3—suggests that outside the United States, the age of youth may go up to 24.) Again, as with children, there may be youth who are involved in activities such as scouting. These youth would be counted only if the thrust of the program was fully a part of the church's educational ministry. A youth is counted only once even if she or he takes part in a variety of goings-on. The GCFA instructions indicate that you count only youth whose participation has been "significant." This is not a comment on the quality of the youth's role; it just means that you number only those who have done more than just pass through.

11c. Number of YOUNG ADULTS CFG participants and leaders (ages 19–30). Some churches have young adult classes whose average age is post-Social Security. "Somehow, we just never got around to changing the name." If you need a working age factor, use 19 to 30 years old. This item is to reflect the ministry in your local context, so students who are away at college would not be counted here even if they are deeply involved in campus ministry (unless, of course, they continue "significant participation" in life at the local church). In helping pastors determine if a small group is primarily about Christian formation, GCFA sees these qualities:

"enhance participants' knowledge and experience of the Bible, spiritual life, and Christian nurture."

11d. Number of other ADULT CFG participants and leaders (ages 31+). As you add up the number of other adults (31 years on up), remember that you should include anyone who is regularly teaching or leading another age group. For example, Lynne Johnson teaches the children's Sunday school class; she would be included in the "other adult" figure, even though her participation is with the younger ones. As mentioned above, each person is counted only once even though they have broad involvements. Sunday school. Bible study. Prayer group. Accountability group (¶ 256.1b). Elsewhere in Table I, there are places to note those engaged in mission projects. In this section, you are focusing on Christian formation.

11. Total CFG participants (11a + 11b + 11c + 11d). Add 'em up. This is the total of Items 11a-d. It tells how many persons from your congregation are engaged in groups for intentional disciple making.

12. Total enrolled in confirmation preparation classes this year. Paragraph 226.4 calls upon the pastor to have confirmation classes for youth to prepare them for professing membership. Of course, you may also have "membership classes" for adults who are moving toward a profession of faith. In this column, you will give the total number of persons who enrolled in such classes, even if they may eventually decide not to become professing members. If they are received on profession of Christian faith, they will also be included in response to Item 2a in Table I.

The next section of entries for Table I will identify the number of participants in CFGs and other small group ministries. This is an effort to determine how many different persons are involved in these activities, so count a participant only once, even if she or he relates to more than one group. (For example, Virginia Fishinger attends an adult Sunday school class, takes part in a midweek Bible study, and leads a weekly prayer group. [Don't tell other pastors about her because they will all try to steal her!] In tabulating the number for "other adults" [item 11d], you would still just count her once.)

Here's an idea: As you complete each of these items, make a note as to how you determined the answer. This will help you the following year and will alert your successor as to how you reached your conclusions.

Prayer: Come, Holy Spirit, and give names to these numbers, that we might find new joy in the journey of faith. Amen.

George's phone rang. After listening for a moment, he remarked to Jacob Lightfoot, "I think Jan Alvarez wants to come over and join us. She is still in the middle of her Table I." "Sure thing," Pastor Jacob grinned. "Like you said, 'We're all in this together.'" It wasn't long until the doorbell rang. The three of them turned to the next report.

Before taking a guess at the answers to numbers 13 to 17, get with someone who is active in the education and formation ministries of the church. Perhaps they will have actual week-by-week records. Perhaps they will have memory of some of the activities. Perhaps they can fill in gaps in your own awareness. (If you serve more than one congregation, there is a good chance that you have not been around, for example, during Sunday church school. You will need the assistance of one of the local church leaders.)

13. Average weekly attendance (all ages) in Sunday school or other weekly education classes. This will test the skills you learned in finger-counting math: simply add the average attendance of each weekly Sunday school class, voilà! Uh, how do you get that information? Perhaps there is a church school superintendent (¶ 255). Perhaps there is someone who tabulates the attendance week-by-week. Perhaps there is an attendance board that announces the figure for each Sunday. Obviously, your task will be well served by having regular records. If you are serving a multi-point charge, you will almost certainly have to depend on someone at each church to gather these statistics for you. If you can do it, your end-of-the-year figuring will be easier if you keep some kind of week-by-week tally. The focus of this item seems to be the traditional Sunday morning education groups.

14. Number of participants in Vacation Bible School. These events (usually in the summer, but at other times where there are year-round schools) are a strong tradition of many churches. The good/bad/challenging news is that Vacation Bible School often takes place just as you move to the new appointment! ("Welcome, Pastor! By the way, will you tell Bible stories to the children each day starting tomorrow?") VBS is often done in conjunction with other congregations; in this report you would give the total number of children involved from all churches. The format may be a full week (or two), an all-day event, or a series of Mondays. The tally you give in this item would be the total number of boys and girls who were participants, not counting anyone twice.

15. Number of ongoing Sunday Church School classes offered. Unless you are on the staff of a large congregation, this datum should be fairly easy to assemble. ("Let's see: children, youth, and two adult classes—that's four.") This column is for reporting those groups that meet weekly on Sunday for at least most of the year. (There is another place—item 17—to record the number of short-term classes.)

16. Number of ongoing small groups, support groups, or classes offered (other than Sunday Church School). Here you would note the number of groups that meet regularly for Christian nurture, but at some time other than Sunday church school. Bible study? Prayer fellowship? Book study group? Small group dynamics? Youth drama team? Children's puppet ministry? Look back at your notes for Item 11d; in that place you are giving the number of people; in this place you are giving the number of groups.

17. Number of support groups or small groups offered for a short term only. Maybe you had a six-week study during Lent. There may be some limited-time groups such as Disciple Bible Study. How about the team you led in studying Christian symbols as they began work on chrismons? Remember the youth met for Bible study every Thursday before going on their summer mission trip? How about the after-school children's prayer warriors that met once a week last September? In response to this point, jot down the total number of such groups over the past year.

18a. Membership in United Methodist Men. The president of United Methodist Men can give you this figure. Paragraph 256.6 calls for each church or charge to have an organized unit of United Methodist Men "chartered and annually renewed through the General Commission on United Methodist Men." You may find that there is an organized men's group on your charge that is not chartered. Ask your district superintendent to advise you as to whether or not to include their membership in this accounting.

18b. Amount paid for projects (UMM). Here you note the total amount the organized men's group has paid for local church and community projects selected by the group. The group's treasurer can give you this information.

19a. Membership in United Methodist Women (UMW). The president of United Methodist Women at your church can give you this number. Paragraph 256.5 speaks of the local church unit of United Methodist Women and how it relates to district and conference and national organizations. If your women's organization is unaffiliated with the connectional United Methodist Women, ask your district superintendent if you should include their membership in this report.

19b. Amount paid for local church and community work (UMW). You can get this total from the treasurer of your local church unit of United Methodist Women. This number is the dollar amount paid for both local church and community projects and programs selected by the group. The figure could contain money sent to other projects and programs chosen by the group, but does not include funds sent to the district or conference for UMW work.

With these financial accountings from United Methodist Men (18b) and United Methodist Women (19b), Table I has begun to shift from nurture to outreach. The last seven items in the table give an indication of local church involvement in mission, outreach, justice, and mercy ministries.

20a. Number of UMVIM teams sent from this local church. UMVIM (United Methodist Volunteers in Mission) is a responsibility of the General Board of Global Ministries (¶ 1302.14). Work teams that go out as UMVIM teams have a leader who has been trained for that role. Most conferences have designated UMVIM coordinators and may even have a special offering for this ministry (¶ 265.5). You will also need to know the number of local church UMVIM teams for a report to charge conference (¶ 247.12). In this column, you do not report on teams that were not affiliated with UMVIM.

20b. Number of persons sent out on UMVIM teams from this local church. Do you have a mission coordinator for the local church (¶ 254)? If so, that person can help you with the information needed for this item. If there is no mission coordinator, ask around: Did the church have a mission trip last year? If so, gather the names of those who went and record the number here. Note: like 20a, this report is only for persons who were on work teams affiliated with United Methodist Volunteers in Mission (UMVIM).

21. Total number of community ministries for outreach, justice, and mercy offered by church. Table I describes this as: Enter the total number of different ministries sponsored by your church (i.e., revivals, community events, food banks, homeless shelters, legal services, community nurse, prison ministry) that are offered to the community as a means of outreach, social justice, and/or mercy.

21a. Of the ministries counted in Line 21, how many focus on global/regional health?

21b. Of the ministries counted in Line 21, how many focus on engaging in ministry with the poor/socially marginalized?

22. Number of persons from your congregation serving in mission/community ministries. Here is a chance to report the total number of individuals who participated in the church's outreach ministries. (This would include folks already mentioned in 20b.) What does it mean to be involved in mission? Take a look at ¶ 256.1c. Also consider this description by the General Council on Finance and Administration: "Ministries that intend to transform people in your local community, the region, and the world . . . any ministry the congregation officially supports, including local food programs, mission teams, disaster response, and/or other mission efforts." A healthy person breathes in and breathes out. A healthy church does the same.

23. Number of persons served by community ministries for outreach, justice, and mercy. This, the final item in Table I (Can I get an "Amen"?), explores how the local church has served others through such activities as homeless shelters, prison visitation, food pantries, preaching missions, blood drives, neighborhood events for social justice, clothing closets, bill payments, and open-door counseling. Your response will be an estimate, but make note of how you came to that number; that will help you and future pastors be able to compare and contrast the effectiveness of these ministries.

 Here's an idea: Use these numbers in your conversation with the church council (¶ 252.1–2) about the local church's programs of nurture, outreach, and mission.

Prayer: Creator God, still creating, stir our hearts so we break the Bread of Life in all the places and among all the people we touch. Amen.

Jan Alvarez and Jacob Lightfoot said thanks to George Baker. The three had pored over Table I, but they did not have time to dig into the remaining work. "The rest of the forms are simple," George teased, "all about finances and property and apportionments and salary and debts and buildings and health insurance and loan payments and budgets and fund-raisers and offerings and custodians. Yes, simple." Jan and Jacob exchanged looks. "Uh, I believe we might be able to stay a little longer," Pastor Alvarez said.

Table II

The items in Table II are in regard to "Church Assets and Expenses." Most of these financial records will be available from the church treasurer or financial secretary. (Just as a side note: no member of the immediate family of the appointed clergy can serve as treasurer, finance chair, financial secretary, counter, or any position under the responsibilities of the committee on finance [¶ 258.4].) Some pastors choose not to know the giving patterns of individuals. Others feel that they need to know in order to deal with the spiritual gift of stewardship.

Occasionally, a pastor runs into a financial officer who does not want to release data the pastor feels is needed for effective leadership. The 2016 General Conference added some language to *The Book of Discipline* regarding one of the duties and responsibilities of the pastor, wording that makes it clear that the pastor has the right to that information if so desired. Let me quote ¶ 340.2c(2)(c) in its entirety: "To provide leadership for the funding ministry of the congregation. To ensure membership care including compliance with charitable giving documentation requirements and to provide appropriate pastoral care, the pastor, in cooperation with the financial secretary, shall have access to and responsibility for professional stewardship of congregational giving records."

24. Market value of church-owned land, buildings, vehicles, and equipment. This total may end up being an estimate. After all, market values change. Include in this figure buildings, equipment, parsonages, and parsonage-related assets. The chairperson of trustees can probably help you.

Last year's figures may be a good starting point for the conversation. One good tool for determining these values is the insurance coverage. (For additional help, look at ¶¶ 2533.2 and 2550.) Because Table II is completed church-by-church, these figures may get complicated for a charge with more than one church. If the parsonage for a multi-point charge is owned by just one of the congregations, list the parsonage-related assets only for the church where the property is located; if, on the other hand, the parsonage property is owned in common by all the churches on the charge—not just one—divide the value among the churches by tabulating each church's percentage of the charge's professing membership. Of course, if some specific percentages have been determined for commonly held property (by the charge-wide conference), that percentage is used to portion out the value to each church's Table II. (I did say this was complicated; I didn't say it was fun!)

25. Market value of financial and other liquid assets. Market value is sometimes hard to figure, so give the best estimate you and other local church leaders can provide. This column would include trust accounts, bonds, stocks, cash, and other properties belonging to the church. Do you have a building fund that is being held for future needs? Does the church own a building that is not used for church purposes? For some settings, this figure is no more than what is left in the checking account. For others, it is a complex accumulation of resources. Note that sometimes a cemetery with historic ties to a church may actually be owned by some non-church entity. Occasionally, local church financial leaders hesitate to be public about the various assets. Paragraph 2550 clearly gives this responsibility for sharing to the local church board of trustees.

26. Debt secured by church physical assets. Does the church have a mortgage or some other kind of debt that is secured by church property or other physical assets? That figure goes here.

27. Other debt. These debts might include church credit cards, a lease-to-purchase agreement, and some other kind of line of credit. If Item 26 and Item 27 are added together, this should represent all of the debts the church owes.

The next information requested begins a number of items about expenditures. At the end of this series, you will add them all together to find the "total amount paid by the local church on all expenditures" (Item 50).

Ever since the day when John Wesley called on the Methodists in London to help pay for a meeting room in Bristol . . . ever since Wesley assigned stewards in each class meeting to gather funds for a pool of money to help the poor . . . ever since Kingswood School in England (1739) and Cokesbury College in America (1784), the people called Methodists contributed to educational ministry . . . ever since the 1853 General Conference of the United Brethren Church set in motion a Missionary Society funded by local societies . . . ever since the followers of Jacob Albright determined in 1803 that evangelical mission was not defined by geography . . . ever since Frances Willard organized other Methodists to join her in crusading against the abuses of alcohol . . . ever since . . . ever since . . . ever since . . . one of the powers in the roots of United Methodism is apportioning local societies and churches a designated share in ministry that could best be undertaken jointly. It is based on the biblical principle (Acts 15:6, Romans 15:16) that we see together better than we see separately. These figures are determined by formulas set by the various conferences (annual, jurisdictional, General), Remember that the word *conference* means "confer." We are in this together.

28a. Amount APPORTIONED to the local church by the CONFERENCE. Get with your church treasurer and add together all the items that the church is expected to pay to the conference treasurer. In some annual conferences, this includes funds to be sent for district expenses; in other conferences, this is paid directly to the district and reported elsewhere (Items 28b and 29b). Typically, Item 28a will include annual conference apportionments for annual conference ministries, jurisdictional apportionments (in the United States) for the work of the jurisdiction—Northeastern, Southeastern, North Central, South Central, Western; general apportionments for the denomination-wide opportunities. This figure may well be the same as the one described in ¶ 247.14: how the district superintendent or designated agent notifies the local church of the apportioned amount.

28b. Amount APPORTIONED to the local church by the DISTRICT (if applicable). Compared to Items 28a and 29b, this line should be easier to figure. The distinction is between any apportionments due to be paid to the district and would not include funds to be paid to the annual conference treasurer.

29a. Amount PAID by the local church to the CONFERENCE for all apportioned causes. As noted in Item 28a, there are annual conferences where district apportionments are paid to the conference treasurer and there are annual conferences where these are paid directly to a district treasurer. (There are annual conferences where there is no such thing as district apportionments.) Keep in mind that for Item 29a; you total only those funds that were paid to the annual conference treasurer. Paragraph 812 reminds us that payment in full of these apportionments "is the first benevolent responsibility of the Church." Your local church treasurer can help you pull together these data.

29b. Amount PAID by the local church to the DISTRICT for all apportioned caused (if applicable). OK. This is the amount actually paid to the district on those items that were apportioned by the district. It does not include anything paid to the conference treasurer or, for that matter, to the pool hall where you work off your tensions after completing these reports.

Here's an idea: At each service where there is an offering, mention and celebrate some connectional ministry being supported by that offering: a home for children, a retirement home, a missionary, a workshop for pastors, a new church start, a conference youth event, a camping ministry, a feeding program, a disaster recovery, spiritual formation events, and so on.

Prayer: Peace-giving God, far-reaching God, grace-filling God, use me as your instrument in leading your people to reach into all the places and people you love. Amen.

---

30. General Advance Specials. These gifts are sometimes called "second-mile giving," because they are beyond the support of apportionment items. Local churches decide which (if any) of these ministries to support. Paragraph 822 describes General Advance Specials. The General Council on Finance and Administration indicates that the annual conference treasurer will provide this figure. In some annual conferences, this may be done by sending information to each local church; in other annual conferences, the treasurer may simply add these figures to the electronic report you file. If this has not been made clear to you, check with the conference statistician or your district superintendent or the conference treasurer.

31. World Service Specials. Read about these funds in ¶ 821. Again, GCFA states that the annual conference treasurer will provide this number.

32. Annual Conference Advance Specials. Annual conferences may establish their own programs that capture the spirit of the "second-mile giving" of Advance Specials. The annual conference treasurer will provide this report.

33. Youth Service Fund. The Youth Service Fund is a way for youth to be engaged in mission projects. The funds, typically raised by the local church's young people, are sent to the annual conference treasurer. The funds then are divided, with 70 percent for distribution as determined by the conference council on youth ministry and 30 percent sent to the general church's ministry with young people. If you want to read more about this, look at ¶ 1208. GCFA notes that the annual conference treasurer will provide the answer to this line item.

34. All other funds sent to Conference for connectional mission and ministry. Without repeating anything already reported in Items 29a–33, this point totals anything else sent to the conference treasurer for other non-apportioned giving. Perhaps this is for disaster relief. Perhaps this is money beyond the apportioned amount for a retirement home or a college. Not to worry: GCFA says that the annual conference treasurer will provide this figure.

35. Annual Conference Special Sunday Offerings. In addition to six churchwide special Sundays that call for an offering (reported below in Items 36a–36f, under the provisions of ¶ 614.5), an annual conference may approve additional special offerings. The annual conference treasurer is to provide this report.

36a. Human Relations Sunday—seeking better human relations throughout the culture.

36b. UMCOR Sunday (formerly One Great Hour of Sharing)—perhaps known in the local church by its former name, "One Great Hour of Sharing," this offering is for direct addressing of human need, particularly in cases of natural disasters.

36c. Peace with Justice Sunday—50 percent used in the annual conference and 50 percent in the general church for ministries that work for "a faithful, just, disarmed, and secure world."

36d. Native American Ministries Sunday—observed in the United States for celebrating and expanding the gifts of Native Americans, both within the annual conference and beyond.

36e. World Communion Sunday—scholarships and programs to help the church move toward inclusiveness.

36f. U.M. Student Day—for scholarships and loans, remembering these words from a Charles Wesley hymn: "Unite the pair so long disjoined, Knowledge and vital piety."

The next several items will be a tabulation of financial information related to your salary and benefits (as well as the same data for other clergy and staff at your local church).

37. Total amount given directly to United Methodist causes (not sent to Conference). If your local church has made contributions directly to a United Methodist institution or cause, get that figure from your church treasurer and put it into this Item 37. The conference treasurer will not have this information because the money did not go through that office.

38. Total amount given to non-United Methodist benevolent and charitable causes. Has your local church given money to some local charity or some community program? A food bank? A homeless shelter? A shelter for abused women? A CROP Walk? A Ronald McDonald House? A chaplaincy program at the hospital? A needy family fund? Because these gifts were not made through the annual conference treasurer, you will need to check with local leadership. Anything sent to the conference treasurer would not be noted on this Item.

39. Total paid for direct-billed and/or non-apportioned clergy pension and other non-health benefits. Your local church or charge treasurer can help you track down these figures. If this amount is deducted from your salary and paid in your behalf, it would not be listed here.

40. Total paid for direct-billed and/or non-apportioned clergy health benefits. This will include any health insurance that is directly billed to the church. The local church or charge treasurer will have this information.

41a. Base compensation paid to/for the Senior Pastor or other person assigned or appointed in the lead pastoral role to the church. This column is for the compensation for the primary pastor (sometimes called senior pastor or lead pastor). Other pastors would be listed in 41b; other staff would be noted in 41c, 42c, and 45. If you have arranged a tax-deferred agreement (IRS 403b) or had contributions made to a "cafeteria plan" (per IRS 125), those amounts are included here. (Don't worry if that doesn't make sense; you will know if you have done this!)

41b. Base compensation paid to/for all Associate Pastor(s) and other pastoral staff assigned or appointed to the church. Include deacons and other clergy in this role. This will be the same sort of figures noted in 41a for the senior pastor; here it applies to any other pastors appointed by the bishop.

41c. Base compensation paid to/for any Deacons not included in 41a or 41b.

42a. Housing benefits paid to/for Lead Pastor or person in lead pastoral role as described in 41a. Note here any payment to you (and associate pastors, if any) for a housing allowance if there is no parsonage provided. This figure will include allowances for housing expenses, such as heating and utilities. If you are in a parsonage, this amount might include utilities paid by the church, ongoing maintenance expense, and furniture. Some congregations give the parsonage family a set amount each year to spend as the family chooses on matters such as small household appliances, decorations, and yard work. If so, this total is listed here. (Be sure it is clear if the purchased item stays with the parsonage or goes with the family.) Any major equipment purchased for the parsonage, significant remodeling, and debts related to the parsonage would be included in 46 and 47.

42b. Housing benefits paid to/for all Associate Pastor(s) and other pastoral staff assigned or appointed to the church. Include deacons and other clergy in this role.

42c. Housing benefits paid to/for any Deacons not included in 41a or 41b.

43. Total amount paid to/for all persons included in Lines 41a–41c for accountable reimbursements. Has the local church reimbursed you for travel expenses? Many congregations allow the pastor funds for continuing education. Has your congregation given you funds for the purchases of books, vestments, organization membership, or publications that are for your personal development? In all cases, these reimbursements should be according to established written agreement with the church (church council minutes, for example) and are to be backed up by receipts or other documentation provided by the pastor.

44. Total amount paid to/for all persons included in Lines 41a–41c for any other cash allowances (non-accountable). If you have been reimbursed for expenses not covered by the accountable reimbursement policy, it goes here. For example, have you been reimbursed but have no receipt? Have you been reimbursed for an item that is not included in the written policy? If so, for tax purposes, these are included in your taxable income; for church reporting purposes, they are listed here. (Do you still have a phone number for a tax consultant? This would be a good time to see if your phone is still working!) The local church treasurer can help you formulate this total.

45. Total amount paid in salary and benefits for all other church staff and diaconal ministers. At one time, The United Methodist Church had a lay office of persons consecrated for service ministries. Although there are no new persons being consecrated to the office, many of those formerly set apart are still serving. Include the salary and benefits totals here for any diaconal ministers employed by your local church. This amount represents what the local church paid for any lay employees (other than diaconal ministers). Salary. Expense reimbursement. Housing. This might include musicians, office staff, custodians, youth workers, children's workers, paid visitors, et al. You are on good terms with the local church treasurer, aren't you? That saint can help you complete this item.

46. Total amount spent for local church program expenses. GCFA defines this as "all amounts spent on local church program for the purposes of education, witness, outreach, mercy, communication, worship, and other ministries." (Monies given to other non-United Methodist agencies are included in 38, not here.) When looking at congregational life during a planning session, you might find it helpful to compare this figure with the same item over a period of time.

47. Total amount spent for other local church operating expenses. Here you will record office expenses, property maintenance, insurance, church utilities, and so on. To avoid double-reporting, make sure none of these amounts has been reported elsewhere. I think the most likely slip-up in reporting twice would be to include something here in 47 and also in 46.

48. Total amount paid for principal and interest on indebtedness, loans, mortgages, etc. Your local church may have borrowed money to build a new fellowship hall. That mortgage is reported here. Your local church might have borrowed money to put floodlights on the steeple. That loan would go here. What does not go here is any item for which you borrowed and then repaid in the current fiscal year. Those amounts go on the lines corresponding to the purpose for which the money was borrowed.

49. Total amount paid on capital expenditures for building, improvements, and major equipment purchases. This line item is for things paid for with contributions, not from borrowed money. (If you collected money for a specific cause, but did not spend it all, note the remainder in line 25.) Did you purchase some "biggie" during the year? An organ? A furnace? A freezer for the kitchen? A life-sized statue of the current pastor? Those kinds of things go on line 49. If you bought the property next door to your building and you paid cash for it from the gifts of the congregation and friends, note that amount here. When you and the treasurer review the checkbook or online account, you will spot the items that go on line 49.

50. Total amount paid by the local church on all expenditures (sum of lines 29a through 49). The easiest way to determine this number is to multiply the number of the nearest interstate highway by the bishop's shoe size and then subtract the number of squirrels seen on church property on May 2. Add this number to the congregation's average worship attendance for 2011.

That is one way to determine this answer. Another way is simply to add 29a through 49.

 Here's an idea: Ever so often, have a member of the congregation give a brief testimony as to how one of the church's financial expenditures has blessed his or her life. Examples might be mission in places he or she could not physically be, learning about the Bible in study groups, a pastoral visit to a hospital, fellowship meals, youth mission trips, child care in the nursery, and so on.

Prayer: Lord Jesus, you reminded us that our hearts go where our treasures are. Help us look at these numbers and learn what you are saying to us. Amen.

George Baker looked over at his pastor colleagues Jan Alvarez and Jacob Lightfoot. The two were playing rock, paper, scissors. It seems that the winner could go home and the loser had to stay to the bitter end. Pastor Baker smiled: "Can I play?" he teased. "From the days of Mr. Otterbein, Mr. Boehm, Mr. Albright, and Mr. Wesley," he began, but before he could complete the sentence, Alvarez and Lightfoot said in unison, "Statistics were one of the signs of accountability and faithfulness." Baker looked pleased. "You remembered!"

Table III

Table III is the final section of these annual reports. It tells the story of church income. How many persons contributed? How much did they give? For what causes was support made? There are three categories of income: (a) received for the local budget (reports 52), (b) received for capital campaigns and other special projects (reports 53), and (c) received from United Methodist and other sources outside the local church (reports 54).

The treasurer has helped you with the information needed for Table II. Now, it is time to check in with the financial secretary (¶ 258.4). Note that in order to avoid even the appearance of a conflict of interest, the positions of treasurer and financial secretary should not be combined and the persons in those offices should not be from the same immediate family. A shorthand way of describing the job descriptions would be: the financial secretary records the income and the treasurer records the outgo.

51. Number of giving units. The financial secretary should have a name for each number recorded here. Remember that ¶ 340.2c(2)c gives you as pastor the right, if you so choose, to have access to these records. If spouses give as one unit, that counts as one; if spouses give separately that counts as two. Children in a household are counted separately if they contribute as separate giving units. The persons reported are those who have during the year given to the local church budget/spending plan and other benevolent causes.

If a congregation shows a deficit in finances, the annual conference can have some appropriate conference committee check into that local church's finances (¶ 604.8). Out of that conversation could come some help for stewardship practices. One of the key items to be explored in such an engagement would be the number of households giving to the local church in comparison to the number of households on the membership and constituency rolls.

The next section of items (52a–g, 52) records monies received for the local church budget or annual spending plan. Do not include funds received from connectional or institutional sources outside the local church (54a–c). Do not include funds designated for specific benevolent causes (53d). Do not include monies used for capital expenditures, unless they were included in the annual budget (53a–d). One is tempted to add: "Do not pass Go. Do not collect $200," but you could probably use the $200, so I won't say that.

52a. Amount received through pledges. If your congregation has some kind of commitment campaign (pledges, estimates of giving), enter here the amount paid toward those commitments. If you do not have such an effort, just leave this line blank.

52b. Amount received from non-pledging, but identified givers. Here you add up the monies received from persons who can be identified but who made no pledge.

52c. Amount received from unidentified givers. Sometimes, this money is referred to as the "loose offering." It is probably the cash put into the offering plate without any identification as to who gave it. It could, of course, include that large stash of one hundred dollar bills that some passer-by left on the church doorstep and left without getting a receipt. (I suppose it would be cheating for me to ask you to send me a receipt for that gift.)

52d. Amount received from interest and dividends and/or transferred from liquid assets. If money from investments or reserve funds is used for the annual budget expenditures, give that amount here.

52e. Amount received from Sale of Church Assets. If the funds received from sale of church assets are used for the ongoing budget, put that on line 52e.

52f. Amount received through building use fees, contributions, and rentals. Are your facilities occasionally rented out for some public function? Does the local church charge for use of the sanctuary for a wedding of a nonmember? Does a day care enterprise rent space in your building? If these funds are used for budget items, give the total amount from such receipts.

52g. Amount received through fundraisers and other sources. Have you had special projects to raise money for the budget? Note these funds here and rejoice that the end of Table III is in sight!

52. Total income for annual budget/spending plan. Add up items 52a through 52g. If your "spending plan" is "to have no plan" (in spite of the injunction of ¶ 252.4c that such a budget is the responsibility of the church council), do the best you can and add up the figures for which you have entries. (Then, put on the agenda of the next church council meeting: "Create a budget.")

Next in the report is an accounting of income received for designated projects. The money that came for projects from the church budget is recorded in 52a–52g and is not repeated here.

53a. Capital campaigns. Here you put the amount received in this year for a capital campaign and any interest received from previous campaign balances.

53b. Memorials, endowments, and bequests. This may be the $25 that was given in memory of Aunt Maude. It might be the $114.27 of interest on an endowment set up by the Percy brothers. Maybe it is $600 that came as a bequest in the will of Xavier Tito. Although the trustees, under the direction of the charge conference, shall handle such bequests (¶ 2533.5), a charge conference can set up a "local church permanent endowment and planned giving ministry committee" to encourage and to act upon these matters (¶ 2534).

53c. Funds from other sources and projects, including sale of buildings. This line item is for receipts from sources other than those already identified. Your finance committee (¶ 258.4) can help you figure out this one.

53d. Amount received for Special Sundays, General Advance Specials, World Service Specials, Conference Advance Specials and other forms of directed benevolent (charitable) giving. These kinds of funds have been noted in items 30–38 as amounts given, but in this line you would give the total of special designated offerings as amounts received. The total in 53d should match the totals of items 30–38. Here you are reporting income; in 30–38 you are reporting outgo.

53. Total income for designated causes including capital campaigns and other special projects. This is one of those "arithmetic columns," simply adding 53a through 53d.

The third section of Table III identifies the amounts of income from United Methodist connectional sources and other institutions.

54a. Equitable Compensation Funds received by Church or Pastor. Ever since the days of Methodism's roots in England, "the people called Methodists" (and their successors) have found ways to support ministries in locales that otherwise might not have a United Methodist presence. Part of conference apportionments (items 28a, 29a) are used to provide salary support in those places (¶¶ 621, 625). If your church has received such compensation help, enter the total year's figure here in item 54a. (And say a prayer of thanksgiving that United Methodist people stick together in ministry.)

54b. Advance Special, apportioned, and connectional funds received by church. Did your local church benefit from denominational funds such as an Advance Special for disaster recovery? Did you get salary support from conference sources other than equitable compensation (for example, funds for new faith communities)? Here is the place to report such monies.

54c. Other grants and financial support from institutional sources. Has an endowment helped your church with hiring an architect for a building project? Did a local cooperative give a grant for your food bank? Have you gotten a grant to take part in a research project? Those kinds of incomes will be reported here.

54. Total income from connectional and other institutional sources outside the local church. Add 'em up: 54a + 54b +54c.

55. Total amount received by the local church. Table III lists this as: (SUM OF LINES 52 + 53 + 54)

And George Baker said, "Thus endeth the lesson." Pastors Alvarez and Lightfoot applauded and thanked their mentor. "By the way," Baker said, "when shall we start working on charge conference report forms?" There was a long silence. Then the two rookies said, "Later. Later."

 Here's an idea: Send an old-fashioned handwritten thank-you note to folks who helped you complete the Table I, Table II, and Table III forms.

Prayer: Lord of the church, help me keep the first things first, so that in all things your name is glorified. Amen.

When John Wesley and Martin Boehm met at the district clergy gathering, they had a good laugh about serving in twenty-first century United Methodism with names that resonated with eighteenth-century clergy of the same names. "There are always those people who think I should be fluent in German," Boehm said. "My best German is 'Gesundheit!'" Wesley nodded in an understanding way. He said, "I wish I had a dollar for every time someone has asked me if my heart was still strangely warmed!" The two got to be good friends and were soon helping each other deal with some of the issues of early time in a first appointment.

What are some of the issues that emerge early on in your appointment? We've already looked at a few and now will explore some others. And, to tell the truth, we shall, no doubt, miss some biggies.

Salary Issues

What do you do if your salary is not paid on time? Paragraph 624 makes it clear that the church or charge is under obligation to pay the base compensation, benefits approved by the annual conference, and any other items adopted by the charge conference. You need to know if payment will be weekly, biweekly, monthly, or on every other third Thursday. If your personal circumstances call for some new arrangement, get the Pastor-Parish Relations Committee (¶ 258.2) to go to bat for you with the treasurer. If you do not get your funds on time, is it just an oversight or is it the temporary unavailability of the treasurer or is it a shortage of funds or is it a deliberate effort to "send you a message"? Obviously, how you handle the situation depends on why it has happened. It may be as easy as a phone call to the treasurer. If there is simply not enough money to keep faith with the financial plan, the Pastor-Parish Relations Committee chair, the treasurer, or the chairperson of the finance committee is to notify you, the congregation, and the district superintendent both in writing and verbally (¶ 624.1). This may lead to annual conference emergency help to meet the need. *The Book of Discipline* is clear (¶ 624.1) that if the compensation has to be reduced, that adjustment is to be made only at the end of the conference appointment year. In other words, you should get what was promised in charge conference action in setting the salary and other compensation (¶ 247.13). If the annual conference has an arrearage policy (¶ 625.2d), that will go into effect if you file a timely claim. If there is no annual conference arrearage policy, civil laws apply. In any case, in order to be eligible for such back compensation as you are due, you must report it immediately in writing to the Pastor-Parish Relations Committee chair, the church council chair, and the district superintendent (¶ 624.2). Be at peace. These kinds of crises are rare.

Disliked by a Member

What do you do when a church member does not like you? Unless we have some psychological issues, most of us want others to like us, or, at least, accept us, or maybe even appreciate us. (If you get your jollies from being disliked, there is a good chance that you will be given many jollies!)

It was over five decades ago, but I still remember the pain and confusion when I realized that everyone in the church did not think I was Mr. Wonderful. It was at a meeting of what then was called the "Official Board." Because we were a newly planted congregation, some in our church family did not have much grasp of "why Methodists give some of their money to the conference." Mr. Vernon—not even close to his real name—raised the question: "Why do we have to pay the apportionments that go to people in other places?" "Well," I said, "for one thing Jesus said we ought to, when he said 'Go therefore and make disciples of all nations.'" Mr. Vernon said nothing, but after the meeting he came up to me: "You insulted me in front of the whole board by quoting Scripture at me in a public meeting!" My reply, in effect, was "Huh?" He never set foot in the church again. I went to visit him at his place of work and he repeated the accusation that I had humiliated him by quoting Scripture at him. He added, "There's nothing else to talk about." Visions of Matthew 18:15-17 rambled through my head. The cautions of James 4:11 seemed very real. The challenge of Hebrews 12:14-15 rattled my confidence. I thought of ways I could have answered differently at that board meeting. I apologized to Mr. Vernon for offending him. I wondered if I had indeed even done anything wrong. Finally, after this self-examination, I told the story to a trusted member of the Pastor-Parish Relations Committee. He said, "Congratulations, you have discovered something important for your ministry; you found out you are not perfect. Now, turn it over to God and get on with it." And I did.

Mountain vs. mole hill? Ego vs. ministry? Popularity vs. faithfulness? Reality vs. dream world? Blame vs. responsibility? Repentance vs. forgiveness. Alas, it is true: not everyone will like you; sometimes it is your baggage; sometimes, it is their baggage; sometimes it is the way your baggages collide. Do what you can, but remember: "Congratulations, you have discovered something important for your ministry; you have found out you are not perfect. Now, turn it over to God and get on with it."

Musical Differences

What if the congregation does not want to sing "I want to be a cowboy for Jesus in the Holy Ghost corral"? First of all—yes, there is a song like that: "I want to do some ropin' of souls now bound for hell and keep them all for Jesus in a Holy Ghost corral."[1] The problem with hymn selection may be simply distaste for the unfamiliar or a lack of appreciation for some musical genre or the limited ability of the accompanist to play or the emotional attachment to long-loved hymns or . . . Here are some ways to address those issues:

(a) Let your musician know in advance about the hymns so she/he can practice or can at least warn you of congregational wariness. (b) There are CDs available from Cokesbury.com for the various official United Methodist hymnal resources; these could supplement or substitute accompaniment that is uncertain. (c) Have a period of time before worship begins to have a hymn sing, inviting members of the congregation to call out favorites they otherwise might not get to sing. (d) Use that pre-service time to practice a hymn that is new for this worshiping community. (e) Have an informal church supper and use that gathering time to teach some new hymns. (f) Offer a hymn sing, perhaps with a visiting friend to help, during which the stories behind hymns are told; there are a number of books available with those stories. (g) Let the choir or a soloist introduce a new hymn by offering it as an anthem or special music. (h) Don't bring too much new hymnody into any one service; include an "oldie-goldie" along with the new one. (i) Be careful not to assume that your musical tastes are the limits of divine inspiration. (j) If a hymn is not "singable," quote it as a poem in your sermon or at some other point in the service. (k) Use hymns as a tool for teaching United Methodist theology. (l) Arrange for children to sing an unfamiliar hymn for the congregation; children can usually win over the most recalcitrant adult singer. (m) Keep a record (maybe marking it in an office hymnal) of each time a particular hymn is used; this will help you avoid wearing out some hymns while ignoring others and it will provide a tool for your successor to know the musical history of the church.

---

1   Ira Stanphill, "A Cowboy for Jesus," ©1948, in *Action Songs for Boys and Girls,* vol. 4, published by Singspiration, ©1955 by Alfred Smith.

(n) Invite a guest to give a concert of hymns, introducing some new ones and enjoying some old ones. (o) Don't assume that everyone knows what is familiar to you; neither contemporary nor traditional hymns are known by everyone. (p) Choose hymns that match the service liturgically, theologically, and thematically. (q) Invite each family in the congregation, in turn, to choose one of the hymns for the worship service. (r) Check with the musician or with the worship committee from time to time to get input and feedback regarding hymn selection. (s) Include a brief—three or four lines—statement in the printed bulletin or projection as to the story behind one of the hymns or maybe even explaining why you chose it. (t) For a change ever so often, have a congregation that usually sings from projected words switch to sing from printed words or vice versa. Ask for feedback and be prepared to duck. (u) Ask the accompanist to play an unfamiliar tune as prelude or offertory or postlude; after this has been done from time to time over a period of months, it has subconsciously become a familiar tune for the congregation and you are ready to match the tune with its words. (v) Ask the congregation to sing a familiar hymn in a different language (for example, for an English-speaking congregation, 59, 191, 228, 239, 344, 378, 583 in *The United Methodist Hymnal*) and ask for shared responses.[2] (w) Use the metrical index in *The United Methodist Hymnal* (926–31) to find a familiar tune that will fit unfamiliar words; your musician can help you locate the appropriate meter (lower right hand corner of each hymn). (x) Have an occasional Music Sunday at the church with the range of musical gifts of the congregation being offered; for the church where I usually worship, such a Sunday might include classical organ, folk music, bluegrass band, children's music, piano solo, older adult choir, chancel choir, soloist, guitarist, saxophonist, drums, and what we lovingly call "The Junk in the Trunk Band." (y) Encourage your members to bring you bulletins from out-of-town services they attend; you may get some good ideas from colleagues that way. (z) You didn't think, did you, that I was going to get this close to "z" without completing the alphabet!

---

2   This has been done at hymn sings. People said it gave them an appreciation of the universality of the gospel, and it helped them realize how hard it can be for many with English as a second language to sing hymns only in English.

Use of Your Time

Do you have to go to everything? How thoughtful of the United Methodist Women to include you in their monthly luncheon! How nice that the United Methodist Youth want you to go with them on their weekend retreat! How inclusive the United Methodist Men are to invite you to help with their all-day Saturday work project! How good it is they want you to be with the children all week at Vacation Bible School! How lovely that both the Baptists and the Presbyterians want you to offer a prayer at their revivals next week! How pleasant that you can be part of the church's semi-annual chicken stew! How charming that the adult Sunday school class wants you to be its regular teacher! How evangelistic that Naomi Dixon, who loves newcomers and is excited about bringing them into the church, gave you the names (and addresses) of three families who are newcomers to the community! How involved you can be now that the Ministerial Association wants you to participate in the downtown protest of a new gambling casino! How wonderful it is to be included in all of the Sunday school classes' Christmas parties! Well, you get the idea.

The demands and pressures on your time can gobble up a full-time load and are even more devastating if you are less than full time, perhaps even while attending Course of Study or seminary or engaged in secular employment. (Someone jokingly suggested that no one be allowed to read ¶ 340 of *The Book of Discipline* [Responsibilities and Duties of Elders and Licensed Pastors] before actually starting the first appointment. Seeing all that is expected before starting might scare away all the potential pastors!) Everything listed in the possibilities noted above is important. So are your health and spiritual well-being and your family opportunities. How do you set priorities? Some of this may come because of your personal interests and spiritual gifts. Some of this may need to be done not because you enjoy it but because relationships are critical to effective ministry. Some of this may be a matter of "This time I'll do A; next time, I'll do B." Some of your priority decisions may shift from time to time as congregational life shifts. Some of the truth is that you may need to find the wisdom and strength to say no thanks.

Here is one way to get some counsel from your Pastor-Parish Relations Committee (¶ 258.2g). Make a list of pastoral activities in a typical week (such as preparing worship, preparing sermon, leading worship, teaching, church fund-raisers, hospital visitation, shut-in visitation, other home visitations, district and conference activities, community events, ecumenical experiences, church social events, counseling, preparing for church council meetings, personal study, mission projects, evangelism, special services—weddings, funerals, justice ministries, dealing with food/clothing/funding ministries, and whatever else you want to add). Print out a copy of this list, perhaps in alphabetical order. Ask each member of the PPRC individually to number these items in order of importance for your pastoral ministry in that place. Collect the sheets and do some tabulating. Out of this ought to come a good conversation starter: What do members of the Pastor-Parish Relations Committee value as your pastoral priorities? You may agree or disagree, but you have the basis for a meaningful dialogue. Then, at a future meeting, ask the PPRC members individually to estimate how many hours you should devote to each of the designated priorities. Figure out the average. How many hours do they expect you to work? (Are there that many hours in a week?) This will again be a tool for getting the committee to "encourage, strengthen, nurture, support, and respect" (¶ 258.2g[1]) you. Note that ¶ 258.2g[4] calls on the PPRC to confer with you on the use of your time, including the time you need for self-care and family life. Our Lord went apart from time to time. Do we dare think we need less time apart than He? The issues here are of spiritual, as well as professional, importance!

Brief Tricks of the Trade

What are some tricks of the trade? Experienced pastors might have some hints to offer about the wheels that can turn a pastoral ministry in a good direction. Here are some you might consider. You will have to decide if they are right for you.

(1) Keep a subject file (electronic or index cards) that will note a quotation that you may want to find again; for example, "Holy Communion: Ryan N. Danker, *Wesley and the Anglicans,* page 181." Obviously, in order to

be helpful you need to hang on to the book being quoted—or make sure you have all the important publishing information copied.

(2) If having a time with children in the regular service of worship is beyond your package of gifts, find a layperson who will handle that for you. You might sit with the children during that time and even join in as seems appropriate.

(3) If the parsonage needs repairs, check with the parsonage committee and/or trustees. They may have a working list of recommended repair people.

(4) Explain any changes you are making in the worship service. Some folks recommend that you make no changes for several months. Many congregations sort of expect a few adjustments when a new pastor arrives. It helps to have a worship committee (¶ 254); then you can say, "The worship committee and I have been talking about our worship life and we'd like to suggest . . ."

(5) Keep your district superintendent's number on your speed dial. Your relationship is going to vary from conference to conference, although all are based on the Constitution (¶ 53), the work of the bishop (¶ 403.2), and the work of the Cabinet (¶ 424). Some districts cover an entire state. Some districts cover no more than an hour's drive. Most D.S.'s do not like to be surprised, so keep her or him informed on life on your charge, especially when things get a bit, shall we say, unusual. You may want the district superintendent to be a pastor to the pastors and one certainly hopes for a pastoral spirit, but the responsibilities of a D.S. do not always allow a comfortable relationship (for example, see ¶ 362.1a about complaints about the character or performance of a clergyperson).

(6) Find out if members of your congregation want notice if you are going to come for a pastoral visit. The PPRC can give you advice about this.

(7) Be careful if you use the church's computer for your internet searches. Is it appropriate to use a church-funded web connection for your personal activities? Have you been less than careful about the sites you visit? Remember: if it goes "out there," your social media and comments and engagements can come back to haunt your ministry.

(8) Is it possible to recognize almost immediately that you misunderstood what you thought was a call from God for pastoral ministry? Active

pastoral work is seldom exactly what we expect it to be. Before you close out the possibility of pastoral service, spend time in prayer, discuss with local church leaders, talk with your local pastor mentor, review matters with your family, and have face-to-face time with your district superintendent.

(9) One of my colleagues has said, "A pastor earns the right to be a prophet in matters of social justice by developing relationships within the congregation." That might mean that your freedom of the pulpit is enriched by the time you spend on social contacts, sharing jokes at a ball game, or stirring the church's traditional Brunswick stew.

(10) The Office of Bishop is established in the United Methodist Constitution (¶¶ 19, 45–54). Read over ¶ 403 and be grateful when you have seen those disciplines in the life and ministry of your episcopal leader. How much direct contact you have with your bishop depends on numerous factors (the geographic area the bishop covers, any special times in the life of your congregation, your service on conference agencies, your participation in district and conference events, and, alas, the necessity of your facing a written and signed complaint accusing you of misconduct [¶ 2702.1]).

 Here's an idea: Use the issues raised in these recent pages as part of your prayer discipline.

Prayer: Shepherd who is also the Lamb, Lamb who is also the Shepherd, watch over my journey so that I do not stray from your flock. Amen.

The First Year

When Babalato Reyes decided to go on a weekend retreat to reflect on her first year in ministry, she asked Barbara Mokma to join her. "Why don't we go to Camp Chestnut, spend some time in prayer, some time in study, some time in silence, and some time in going over this past year?" "I need that," Pastor Mokma answered. "I know some of it has gone well and some not so well. Let's look at Year Number One. There won't be another 'first year.'"

Basics of Leadership

There is an old saying: "You ain't leading, if nobody's following." By the time a year has passed, you will likely be aware that leadership is not an automatic function of an office, but is a matter of the grace-touched exercise of the basics in relationships. "As God's chosen ones, holy and beloved, clothe yourselves with compassion, kindness, humility, meekness, and patience" (Colossians 3:12). Those are the basics of leadership. Other words that show up in this Pauline injunction include forgive, love, peace, teach, admonish, wisdom, gratitude, sing . . . "And whatever you do, in word or deed, do everything in the name of the Lord Jesus, giving thanks to God the Father through him" (Colossians 3:17).

Nominations and Leadership Development

One of the critical roles for the pastor of a local church is chairing the Committee on Nominations and Leadership Development (¶ 258.1) This committee prepares a slate of nominations for the consideration of the charge conference in electing church officers. (Nominations may also be made from the floor.) Use the index of *The Book of Discipline* to find descriptions of the responsibilities of the various required offices.

It is helpful for this committee also to meet throughout the year, dealing with such questions as: What new leadership positions do we need? What training and development is available for our leaders? How well are persons functioning in their responsibilities? Are one or two persons covering so many positions that others do not have a chance to serve? What changes in leadership might be fruitful in the coming year? Have vacancies occurred among our leadership positions (¶ 252.4b)? How have we taken seriously the gospel's commitment to inclusivity and diversity (¶ 258.1e)? Some pastors seek to avoid a perceived conflict of interest by not engaging in discussion of who should be nominated for the Pastor-Parish Relations Committee—although it's permissible.

One of the most tender issues that can emerge for this committee is handling a situation in which one person has a longtime hold on a position, when it seems to many that a change would be best for the mission of the church. These transition plans should probably be handled by a team from the committee, unless there is some special relationship that suggests otherwise. How have others approached this? (1) One way, of course, is a direct conversation with the individual. Some persons are actually eager to let go of a responsibility, but have hung on simply out of a sense of obligation. For some, it is a matter of self-identity and to lose an office is painful to their sense of self-worth. This approach calls for deep pastoral sensitivity. (2) Another method of initiating a change is to alter the job description. The officeholder may not want to tackle the new way of handling things and will offer to step aside. (3) Perhaps the problem area could be put into a separate position; the recalcitrant member could still hold the coveted title, but would not be responsible for what she or he had not been able to handle. (4) Perhaps a giant celebration "honoring Liam Forsyth for his forty-seven years as Sunday school superintendent" would signal the time for a change. (5) Invite the individual in question to have a cochairperson or an assistant, "someone you could be training so this ministry will go on." (6) Ask the newly elected person to seek the wisdom of the predecessor. (7) Get the charge conference to implement ¶ 247.7, limiting how long a person can be in an office.

Holy Communion

Most pastors remember the first time they presided at a service of Holy Communion. It is indeed a remarkable and humbling thing to be trusted with the sacraments of the church. The two sacraments that United Methodists recognize (baptism and Holy Communion—¶ 104, Article XVI Methodist, Article VI EUB) belong to the whole church, but only certain members are authorized to administer at the Table and to baptize (¶ 316.1). I think of it like this: Suppose a family gets a Christmas gift addressed to the whole family; on Christmas morning they turn to one of the children and say, "This belongs to all of us, but we want you to open it." Some of this understanding is rooted in Paul's New Testament call for order (1 Corinthians 14:40, for example). The ordained or licensed pastor represents the "handed on" tradition of the church and connects the gathered body to the worldwide body of Christ, both historic and present.

If you are ill-at-ease as you get ready for your first time as pastor at the Table, review pages 27–31 of *The United Methodist Book of Worship*. There you will find step-by-step procedures for each of the four actions of the Lord's Supper (Take, Thank, Break, Give). As suggested for your first worship service, it is a good idea to do a "walk through" of the Communion ritual in your worship space.

Early on in your appointment, connect with the designated Communion steward. (This is the person who prepares the elements and arranges the Communion table.) Is the Communion bread gluten-free? If not, is there a provision of gluten-free bread for those whose bodies cannot tolerate gluten? (There are usually bakery sources for gluten-free bread and there are recipes online.) Will someone help you serve the elements? Is the tradition at this church to kneel to receive Communion? Is there a chalice or are there individual cups? Does the congregation sing hymns as persons are served? Are there members who need to be served where they are seated? Do some members decline to take Communion? Are the elements presented as part of the offering or are they already on the Table? How often has Communion been offered? Is there a provision for taking Communion to shut-ins? After Communion, what happens to the remaining elements? (See p. 30 of *The Book of Worship*.)

Some pastors have been surprised (at the last minute!) when they uncovered the elements only to discover that instead of the traditional grape juice there was homemade raspberry juice, full-strength wine, or, as one reported, Coca-Cola. Perhaps, if it seems appropriate, you can review with congregational leaders these words from *The Book of Worship* (p. 28): "Although the historic and ecumenical Christian practice has been to use wine, the use of unfermented grape juice by The United Methodist Church and its predecessors since the late nineteenth century expresses pastoral concern for recovering alcoholics, enables the participation of children and youth, and supports the church's witness of abstinence." There is further comment on the bread and cup ("grain and grape," as my pastor calls it) in *The Book of Resolutions of The United Methodist Church 2016*, pages 761–64. (Yes. It is true. Welch's Grape Juice was begun in the nineteenth century by a Methodist dentist who wanted to provide unfermented sacramental wine. Check out the story on the internet.)

The Book of Worship notes that "We have no tradition of refusing any who present themselves, desiring to receive" (p. 29). If neither you, as the appointed pastor, nor an ordained elder is present to preside, the congregation should choose to have a Love Feast instead of Holy Communion (see pp. 581–84 of *The Book of Worship*).

If you want to explore the full richness of the practice of Holy Communion in The United Methodist tradition, read *This Holy Mystery.* It is the official statement of United Methodist understanding of the Eucharist (as Holy Communion is sometimes called). This resource is available as a separate booklet; it is also printed in full in *The Book of Resolutions*. You can also download it here: https://www.umcdiscipleship.org/resources/this-holy-mystery-a-united-methodist-understanding-of-holy-communion.

Here's an idea: If you want to help your congregation move toward more frequent Communion, perhaps you could begin by offering it weekly during some limited season of the church year—Lent or Advent, for example.

Prayer: Lord of the church, be with us in your Real Presence so our decisions, our life together, and the Holy Table may be made alive with your grace. Amen.

———————

As Pastors Reyes and Mokma sat looking over the lake at Camp Chestnut, they enjoyed the quiet and the scenic beauty. Each one was absorbed in her own thoughts. Babalato Reyes broke the silence. "Barbara," she began with some hesitancy. "Can I share something rather personal with you? I need to tell somebody." Pastor Mokma looked over at her friend. A slight smile was creeping across Babalato's face. "Sure! Tell me whatever you want to." The grin on Babalato Reyes's countenance said volumes: "I think I've fallen in love with a man in my congregation."

Falling in Love

Yes, pastors can have a love life. The disciplinary boundaries of "fidelity in marriage and celibacy in singleness" (¶ 304.2, ¶ 2702.1a) may narrow, but do not eliminate, the possibilities. There are many relationships that can, as one person put it, "appropriately increase the heart rate." That's a semi-poetic way of saying "I'm in love."

Apart from the obvious integrity issues of the marital status of the two parties and apart from the moral decisions about the sexual content of the association, there is for a pastor an additional dimension: Is this person a member of your congregation?

It is easy to understand why a pastor might fall in love with a congregant. They are together frequently. They have common interests. And they are "available." What's the problem? Cupid has certainly had worse aim in the past.

The operative words here are "member of your congregation." Pastoral relationships have what observers call "a power differential." You may not feel that power, but it goes with the territory, what professionals call "role power." Personal relationships, on the other hand, survive and flourish when there is a balance in the proportions of power. To confuse these two kinds of relationships is to complicate both the pastoral and the personal proportions. Your "friend" is left without a full pastor. One option, of course, is to cool the personal contact. Another option is to encourage "the other" to find pastoral support in another congregation, so your relationship can develop in healthy ways. Of course, a third option is to ignore these warning flags and be madly in love with this wonderful member of your congregation.

This awareness of pastoral boundaries has emerged in recent years. An informal poll at one district meeting I attended revealed that well over half of the pastors had met their spouses in a church they were serving. Seeing the potential of harm that can come from the role power differential and observing the dangers of relationships that were based on a misperception of a pastor's caring spirit and understanding the tensions, sometimes unspoken, that can occur when "favoritism" is seen in some pastoral connections—all of this leads to a word of caution: falling in love is a grand thing; ignoring pastoral boundaries is not. (Full disclosure: I met my wife in the congregation where I was an associate pastor; the senior minister served as her pastor. If I was wrong in pursuing the relationship with Toni, I was happily wrong for almost fifty-two years.) Despite the wonders of love, take caution! It is a bad idea to date anyone who remains in your congregation. When things went awry in such a situation, some have lost their appointment; some have lost their reputation; and some, alas, have lost their clergy credentials.

Pastoral Care for Your Family

There is a side concern that surfaces in these thoughts. How does a pastor's family get pastoral care? In many ways, family members participate and benefit from the ongoing life of the parish. If your appointment is to an extension ministry, you have no doubt related to a charge conference; the pastor there is your family's pastor. If a family member would profit from a counseling relationship, check to see if your annual conference has a counseling and psychological services ministry. If not, your health insurance plan probably covers the cost of such therapy in another setting. Can a colleague provide a referral? Is there a trusted friend who can provide an ear? How about a pastor in another denomination? Keep in mind that these are also options for you when you yourself need such counseling. There is no shame in getting help; the shame is in ignoring help that is available.

Sexual Exploitation

When I see a newspaper or internet headline that says "Pastor Accused of Abusing Church Youth," I rush to read the story with two questions: "Is it someone I know? Is it a United Methodist?" Sadly, sometimes the answer is yes.

Sexual abuse and sexual harassment are two forms of "exploitation of a power relationship" (Social Principles, ¶ 161 J). The adjectives used in *The Book of Discipline* to describe these inappropriate sexual expressions are "exploitative, abusive, or promiscuous" (¶ 161 I). Only the most broken of persons would set out deliberately to hurt another in these ways, but the power of misplaced ego and undisciplined sexual urges and the ease with which we fool ourselves blur into destructive relationships. If these temptations knock on your door, take care not to be in settings where you give in to such base desire. Guard your fantasy life so it does not seem natural to violate those pastoral (and simply human) boundaries. Those violations are subject to charges (¶ 2702.1) within The United Methodist Church and possibly in civil law.

If you struggle with these sexual pressures, seek confidential counseling. Your ministry is at stake and your spiritual journey is at risk.

Here's an idea: Review the sections "Falling in Love" and "Sexual Exploitation" and then jot down what seem to be the two most important sentences. Let these sentences be a focus of your prayer life for the next week.

Prayer: Holy Spirit, bring me your wisdom and your abiding presence, that I might live into holiness. Amen.

District Superintendent Ashley Peterson looked at the room filled with unsmiling faces. "Thank you for coming today," the D.S. began, "because getting charge conference right is super important. Shall we begin?"

Charge Conference

For starters, having a charge conference is a constitutional requirement of The United Methodist Church: "There shall be a charge conference for each church or charge with such powers, duties, and privileges as are hereinafter set forth" (¶ 12, Article V). Even with that overarching statement, what charge conferences look like can vary greatly from annual conference to annual conference and even within a single annual conference. For example, the district superintendent may preside or may designate another elder to preside (¶ 246.5). For example, your charge conference may be part of a joint charge conference in which the worship time is shared with other churches, but business takes place in separate spaces. For example, your charge conference business may be conducted in the same time/room as other churches, taking moments for the votes required by each church (¶ 246.10). For example, your charge conference may meet as a church conference, in which case the vote is extended to all professing members of the church who are present (no proxies) (¶ 248). For example, your charge conference may meet in a special session called by the district superintendent, with no other business conducted other than what is mentioned in the call (¶ 246.7). For example, some annual conferences require reports to be in writing; some annual conferences ask that they be filed electronically; in some annual conferences, some response forms are printed and others are to be sent in electronically. Your district superintendent or conference website will have instructions for your situation.

In this space, I'll not duplicate all of what is spelled out about the charge conference in *The Book of Discipline*. The basic text is found in ¶¶ 246–51. (Let me suggest that you read a paragraph aloud at the breakfast table each morning. This will help you be up-to-date and it will make your family dog well informed about United Methodist matters.) What I shall do in these next few reflections is to comment on some of the dimensions that can be troublesome.

Pastor's Vote

Should I vote? You are a member of the charge conference (¶¶ 246.2, 252.5 l). You have the right to vote on all matters, although voting on your salary would be an obvious conflict of interest. Some pastors choose not to vote on any items before the charge conference, thus avoiding the risk of taking sides on controversial decisions. On the other hand, it may be important that pastoral leadership be seen as supportive of the choices being made by the charge conference; on the other hand (does that make three hands?), what happens to your ministry as pastor if you are seen voting on a non-prevailing side? On yet another hand (are we up to four?), you may see it as your pastoral and prophetic role to identify with an unpopular but justice-driven cause. Weighing all these options leads some pastors to refrain from voting at all. Can I confuse the matter a bit more? The introductory paragraph for ¶ 246 indicates that all members of the charge conference shall be "professing members of the local church," but then specifically names the pastor as an exofficio member and indicates later (¶ 246.2) that retired ordained pastors and retired diaconal ministers are indeed members of a charge conference; their professing membership is in the annual conference, not the local church. The evident confusion is the only place in the history of Christendom where there has been such confusion. Hmmm.

Rationale for Charge Conference

Why bother? Why not let the church council handle all this business and do away with the charge conference? The answer is straightforward and named in ¶ 247.1: "The charge conference shall be the connecting link between the local church and the general Church . . ." The charge conference is a reminder that local churches do not exist in isolation; we are part of a connectional journey. The charge conference symbolizes the biblical principle that our life in Christ is held in common: Acts 4:32, 11:22, 15:2;

Romans 15:25-26. The charge conference lives out the principle that major local church decisions (election of officers, share in connectional ministries, compensation for appointed clergy, building projects, etc.) are, in truth, decisions that affect the entire denomination. The charge conference is a checkpoint to determine if the ministry and mission of the church council are in keeping with the objectives of The United Methodist Church (¶ 247.3). The charge conference offers potential clergy to the rest of the connection (¶ 247.8). The charge conference identifies lay servant ministers who might be eligible for recognition by the district and conference committee on Lay Servant Ministry (¶ 247.11). It is more than a convenience that the district superintendent or an elder designated by the district superintendent presides at the charge conference; that requirement is a sign that the local church, at the charge conference, is holding hands with other United Methodists around the world.

Annual Audit

Whose business is it as to how much money we have? *The Book of Discipline* (¶ 258.4d) requires the local church committee on finance to provide the charge conference with "a full and complete" audit of the financial accounts of the local church. In some annual conferences, this report can be filed electronically; in other annual conferences it is submitted on an official audit paper form. Occasionally, the financial officers of a congregation resist having such an audit being made public. The concern is usually not because of some illegal or nefarious activity but because there is some feeling of loss of control if "everybody knows how much money we have." That "everybody" often means the annual conference. A few local church committees on finance fear the annual conference will "pounce" if it discovers the true resources of that congregation. Such distrust is ill-founded.

The audit need not be done by a professional (although that is an option, of course); it might be simply an independent review by a committee of persons who are not related to the people directly connected to the financial accounts. (See ¶ 258.4d for examples of those who might be considered linked to the finances.) If not filed and shared generally, the audit report should be available to any member of the charge conference who wants to see it. The integrity of the finances of the local church is a matter of stewardship, self-control, generosity, faithfulness, community. That is beginning to sound like the fruit of the Spirit (Galatians 5:22)!

Removing Professing Members

It's a sad duty. It is sometimes the difficult and unhappy responsibility of the charge conference to remove the name of a professing member from the official roll of the local church. This might be someone who does not participate in the "active fellowship of the church," in spite of the consistent effort of the church council to make that happen. This might be a professing member who has moved and made no connection with a congregation in his or her new community. This might be a professing member whom no one knows or whose address is lost. There is no joy in implementing the provisions of ¶ 228.2b[4], but to fail to do so might well reflect a failure to take seriously what professing membership means. That disciplinary paragraph has several safeguards to make sure this action of removing a professing member from the roll is not done casually or with haste. Before the charge conference votes to remove the name, the pastor and evangelism chairperson must recommend such action. If there is more than one name, the names are to be considered one at a time. In order to be considered, the name should have been entered into the minutes of two consecutive charge conferences. Keep in mind that there are provisions for restoring these persons to membership.

Approving Potential Candidates for Ministry

It's a glad duty. If the local church Pastor-Parish Relations Committee so approves, the charge conference may recommend persons to the district committee on ordained ministry for certification as candidates for licensed or ordained ministry (¶ 310.1e). Perhaps you have recently gone through these steps yourself. *The Book of Discipline* spells out a daunting list of qualities desired in those seeking to become candidates (¶ 310.1d). Often, these potential candidates are asked to address the charge conference about their call to ministry. Members of the charge conference may have questions for the proposed candidates. This should not be routine business. In order to assure the freedom of members of the charge conference to vote without concern for disrupting future relationships, the vote is to be by written ballot. Two-thirds of the charge conference must approve. Almost always, this is an occasion for celebration and encouragement. If, on the other hand, the charge conference has by its vote said no or maybe later or not ready, you will need to draw upon your own pastoral strengths to help the denied candidate process this disappointment.

Nominations from the Floor

Are there any nominations from the floor? This is usually a slam dunk. The committee on nominations and leadership development presents its report. The presiding elder asks if there are any nominations from the floor. There is no response and then the slate gets elected. Not so fast! Every so often, there is indeed an additional nomination from the floor. Then, the vote is taken, typically with no one bent out of shape. In a rare situation—by rare, I mean it happened to me once in my six years as a district superintendent with about 350 charge conference sessions—persons who are discontented with church leadership may propose a new nomination for every one offered by the committee on nominations and leadership development. Talk about awkward. As pastor, you have chaired the committee whose report is under attack. However, also as pastor you are going to have to work closely with anyone elected, including those nominated from the floor. That would be a good time to commit Hebrews 12:14-15 to memory and to heart.

 Here's an idea: Go over the items needed for charge conference (list probably provided by your district superintendent); note who is responsible for each report; schedule a time with each one to double-check readiness.

Prayer: Lord of the church, you have prayed before the One you called Father and asked that all your people be one. Lord, make it so. Amen.

Eul Kim, Julia Worthington, and Terry Dickinson met every Wednesday morning for breakfast. It was a time for what they called "holy gossip." On one such morning, Julia showed up with her own version of "United Methodist Trivia." It led to a combination of laughter, teasing, argument, and information.

United Methodist Trivia

Let's try some United Methodist Trivia:

Q: Does The United Methodist Church exist?

A: No. According to ¶ 141: "Under the Constitution and disciplinary procedures set forth in this *Book of Discipline*, 'The United Methodist Church' as a denominational whole is not an entity nor does it possess legal capacities and attributes."

Q: What are the constitutional bodies for the entire United Methodist Church?

A: General Conference, Council of Bishops, Judicial Council.

Q: From 1784 to 2016, how many persons have been elected bishop in The United Methodist Church and its predecessor bodies?

A: 615—if I counted correctly!

Q: Which bishop has the longest last name?

A: It's a tie. In 1845, Jacob John Glossbrenner was elected; in 1980, Louis Wesley Schowengerdt was elected. (There are several with only three letters in the last name.)

Q: How many pages are in the 2016 *Book of Discipline*?

A: There are 898 numbered pages.

Q: How many pages are in the 1798 *Doctrines and Discipline of the Methodist Episcopal Church in America*?

A: There are 198 numbered pages.

Q: What does that great difference in number of pages mean?

A: No comment.

Q: What is the subject matter of the very last paragraph in *The Book of Discipline*?

A: It is a statement about which edition of *The Discipline* shall be used in the process of a judicial procedure when a complaint has been forwarded to the counsel for the Church.

Q: Which is correct: "the United Methodist Church" or "The United Methodist Church"?

A: The United Methodist Church.

Q: What are the five jurisdictions within the United States?

A: Northeastern, Southeastern, North Central, South Central, and Western.

Q: Which of these countries do not have a United Methodist congregation: Liberia, England, Russia, Canada, Philippines, Austria, Denmark, Ukraine, Finland, Hungary, Zambia?

A: England (The main Methodist body is The Methodist Church in Great Britain.) and Canada (Methodists and Evangelical United Brethren are now part of The United Church of Canada.).

Q: Which annual conference had the most delegates for the 2016 General Conference?

A: Nigeria Annual Conference had thirty delegates. The two largest delegations from the United States were North Georgia Annual Conference and Virginia Annual Conference, each with twenty-six delegates.

Q: Why do all delegations to the General Conference have an even number of delegates?

A: Each has an equal number of lay and clergy delegates.

Q: How many United Methodist seminaries are there? How many can you name?

A: There are thirteen. They are Boston, Candler (Emory), Claremont, Drew, Duke, Gammon, Garrett-Evangelical, Iliff, Methodist, Perkins (SMU), Saint Paul, United, and Wesley.

Q: How many predominantly Native American United Methodist congregations are there? Which state has the most Native American United Methodist professing members?

A: There are 111 predominantly Native American congregations in the United States. North Carolina has the most such ministries.

Q: What happens to the net income from The United Methodist Publishing House (Cokesbury is the retail division)?

A: According to the Constitution (¶ 22), these funds are used only for beneficiaries of the ministerial pension systems.

Q: What is the most frequently used first word in hymn titles in *The United Methodist Hymnal*?

A: There are fifty-two hymns whose title (usually the first line) begins with "O."

Q: Of these three key figures in the early days of predecessors of The United Methodist Church, which one came to America first: Francis Asbury, Barbara Heck, or Philip William Otterbein?

A: Otterbein (1752 from Germany), Heck (1760 from Ireland), Asbury (1771 from England).

Q: What was Susanna Wesley's name before she married Samuel Wesley? (They are John Wesley's parents.)

A: She was Susanna Annesley.

 Here's an idea: Use these (and other) quick trivia questions in a church newsletter or bulletin as a way of introducing United Methodist history and practice.

Prayer: God of bountiful grace, we are not the first to call you Lord. Bring Your Spirit upon our ministries so that we shall not be the last. Amen.

Locklear Longwalker, Barbara Elliott, and Murray Turner were excited to begin their assignment: Bring to the next sub-district meeting of clergy some ideas about fund-raising in the local church. Now that each one had finished one year under appointment, they had plenty of fuel for that fire! Longwalker had been the associate pastor of a large membership congregation; Elliott had been appointed to a nonprofit hunger relief organization; Turner had served as pastor of three part-time churches. "It's all about tithing." "You've got to have big givers to set the pace." "If people are strong spiritually, they will be strong in their giving." This was going to be an interesting conversation!

Fund-Raising

The Bible speaks of a tithe (one-tenth) as one way to give to God (Genesis 28:22, Leviticus 27:32, Malachi 3:8) and yet the Bible also says that tithing is not enough (Matthew 23:23, Luke 11:42). One of the highest words of praise that Jesus ever gave was when he described a widow who had put two small coins into the offering (Luke 21:1-4). And then there is that troublesome time when Jesus told a rich man to sell everything he had and to give the money to the poor (Mark 10:17-22). Perhaps it all balances out in the end because Paul wrote Timothy, "we brought nothing into the world, so that we can take nothing out of it" (1 Timothy 6:7). That's just before Paul admonishes the young Timothy to remember that "the love of money is a root of all kinds of evil" (1 Timothy 6:10). There are few, if any, topics in Scripture that get more attention than issues of wealth, of stewardship, or worldly resources. Is it a coincidence that it was the treasurer of the disciples' money who was tempted into betraying Jesus (John 13:29)? How do we deal with the reality that early Christians put all their resources into a common pool (Acts 2:43-44)? Should financial records be kept secret (Matthew 6:3)? Does God promise to take care of those who give to the poor (Proverbs 28:27)? And doesn't the Scripture tell us that the gifts of God are free (Isaiah 55:1)? Oh, yes. Let's not forget the in-your-face words of Jesus: "You cannot serve God and wealth" (Luke 16:13). That must be true, because it is in red ink in the Bible on my desk. The coming of God in flesh in Jesus has made this world a place of divine revelation (John 1:14). Now if we can just figure out what that means for fund-raising in the local church.

Is paying the light bill part of the church's ministry? How about money that is gathered to help victims of a tornado? Decorating the parsonage? Materials for the children's Sunday school class? Floodlights so the church steeple can be seen at night? How about employing a part-time custodian? Building a playground so neighborhood youth can play soccer? Apportionment money that goes to start a new congregation on the other side of the state? And so on? Clearly, the work of developing a plan for spending the church's money is a complicated task, even if there is not much money to spend!

The Book of Discipline (¶¶ 252.4c, 258.4) assigns this budgeting responsibility to the church council, acting on recommendations from the committee on finance. As "administrative officer" of the local church, you have a place in those processes (¶ 244.3). These steps include not only how to spend resources but also how to raise funds.

Some congregations have long-established patterns for fund-raising. Varying the processes from time to time may tap new resources. You might want to encourage an emphasis on the spiritual dimension of what it means to be a steward of God's creation. The development of faithful stewardship is a year-round venture, not just something to be attended to during a financial campaign. Sometimes, a special weight is needed for a special project, for example, a new building, establishing an endowment, getting the carpet cleaned, supporting a mission team, buying a computer and printer for the church, getting the organ refurbished, an unexpected need in the community, or a sign in front of the church building. The principles of the New Testament church regarding finances include such words as "pleased to share" (Romans 15:26), "on the first day of every week" (1 Corinthians 16:2), and "begging us earnestly for the privilege" (2 Corinthians 8:4). What are some ways to live out these biblical descriptions in today's local churches?

Church A: This congregation just pays its bills with no plan in place other than "Folks, we are a little short this week."

Church B: This church sets its budget (¶ 252.4c) and then sends out notices to all the professing members, asking them to make pledges toward meeting that budget. If the pledges fall short, the budget might get revised. (They order the stewardship pledge cards from Cokesbury.com and collect them on a designated Sunday.)

Church C: Before establishing the budget for the next fiscal year, this congregation asks for pledges from the professing members. They then add in an amount equal to what they can expect from unpledged giving. That total becomes the bottom line of the budget that will then be prepared.

Church D: In an effort to make sure everyone is onboard, a stewardship team visits neighborhood groups (families and individuals go to a centrally located home in the neighborhood) and after exploring the spiritual dimensions of giving, they describe the proposed budget. They give each family pledge cards to be turned in on Stewardship Sunday.

Church E: For several weeks leading up to a Commitment Sunday, professing members give brief testimonies about what they value in the church budget.

Church F: For several weeks leading up to a Commitment Sunday, professing members tell how they reach their personal giving decisions.

Church G: The pastor conducts a Bible study about Jesus' teachings about money.

Church H: This church, thinking that perhaps an outsider can raise important but difficult questions, asks the conference to recommend someone to help them conduct a financial campaign.

Church I: Recognizing that there is a plus and a minus in doing so, the pastor shares with the congregation exactly how much the pastor's family gives to the church, thus perhaps leading by example.

Church J: All year long, this church shows a brief video every Sunday, highlighting both local and worldwide ministry supported by the church budget. (The youth might jump at the chance to produce this video.)

Church K: With funds needed for both the ongoing budget and for a building program, these people provide offering envelopes that have designated giving boxes: (a) budget, (b) building fund.

Church L: On a Commitment Sunday when estimate-of-giving cards are presented by the membership, this community stays in place until the totals are added up. If it is not enough to meet the budget, the membership is asked to increase its pledges.

Church M: The financial secretary maintains a careful record of how much money was contributed from persons who pledged and how much was contributed in loose offerings without connection to a pledge. This information helps the church council make budget plans.

Church N: Needing money for a major one-time project (such as replacing a flat roof with a peaked roof), this group borrows the money from a local bank and conducts a campaign to raise one-time gifts and pledges to meet the payments. Sometimes, a bank will require that this fund-raising effort precede the loan.

Church O: Remembering something that works well in another church, this pastor arranged for the church officials to meet with a representative of a company that specializes in selling bonds for huge local church projects.

Church P: One way this congregation has helped children and youth learn about giving is to see that each child and each youth has her or his own set of envelopes for regular giving.

Church Q: Aware that many people now use automatic withdrawals to pay bills and to make contributions, this church developed an electronic system so members could have funds automatically sent to the church each month or each week.

Church R: This large membership congregation put an ATM machine in a discreet place at the church, so persons could get cash to put into the offering plate.

Church S: At its contemporary service, this group simply had a basket at the door, so persons could make gifts as they leave the service. They are careful to anticipate these gifts by singing doxological music during the service.

Church T: This congregation had a division between those who wanted the offering received in the middle of the service and those who wanted it as a closing act of worship. They compromised: the offering was received in the middle of the service, but it was not presented at the Table until a Doxology followed the closing hymn.

Church U: After receiving a number of memorial gifts, this church created a "Memorial Fund" and unless the gift was designated for some specific cause (¶ 258.4f), the money went into the Memorial Fund. The church council had the authority to spend those funds.

Church V: Originally intended to raise money for specific projects or simply to boost the budget income, this group held an apple butter fundraiser twice each year. What they discovered was that the fellowship in a common project meant as much (or more) than the money raised. (Some years, they combined this project with a yard sale.)

Church W: With a social media savvy membership, these people used Facebook, YouTube, and a website to tell the congregation's story. They even tried some of the online fund-raising programs.

Church X: This congregation has a fellowship supper each month and asks those who come to donate, if they can, enough to cover the cost of the meal "plus a little something extra." Occasionally, a generous member will offer to match the receipts for that month's meal.

Church Y: Every year, just before Valentine's Day, a member of this congregation takes orders for home-baked cookies and gives all of the income to the church. Some years, she designates that the funds will go for apportionments (¶ 812).

Church Z: This church offered a program on "The Meaning of Biblical Tithing." In addition to Bible study, a panel discussed whether a tithe was on gross income, net income, taxable income, or something else. Does money given only to the church count as part of the tithe or can the tithe include any charitable contribution?

Church AA: Ha! You thought I'd stop at Church Z! Here's another reflection on fund-raising: The person doing the weekly bulletin includes the amount needed to date and amount received to date and other such financial data. Church AA also makes a comparison with this year to date and last year to date.

Church AB: This group had a series of nine services based on the nine fruits of the Spirit noted in Galatians 5:22-23. The week that focused on generosity involved children making posters for the church bulletin board, youth donating their time in helping elderly members with yard work, adults following a daily devotional discipline, and a congregation-wide collection of time, talent, and money promises.

Church AC: Each time this congregation receives a new member, they have professing members prepared to give a brief testimony about each of the vows made by the new member: prayers, presence, gifts, service, and witness.

Church AD: Although some considered it a bit "in your face," this church ran a note all summer in the bulletin and projected the announcement: "God has not taken a vacation; be sure your offering has not."

Church AE: This historic congregation kept this quotation from John Wesley posted: "If (when I die) I leave behind me ten pounds (above my debts and the little arrears of my fellowship) you and all mankind (may) bear witness against me that 'I lived and died a thief and a robber.'"

Church AF: Once when preaching on Luke 16:1-13, the pastor of this congregation quoted John Wesley's sermon "The Good Steward": "We are not at liberty to use what he has lodged in our hands as *we* please, but as he pleases, who alone is the Possessor of heaven and earth, and the Lord of every creature."

Church AG: Recognizing that members had varying financial situations, the stewardship committee of this church encouraged people who were not ready yet to tithe (10 percent) to discipline their giving by being systematic in whatever they are able to do.

Church AH: The charge conference established a local church permanent endowment and planned giving ministry committee (¶ 2534). This committee helped members move toward including the church in their wills and bequests and estate plans. They found resources under Leadership Resources at umcdiscipleship.org, and they conferred with their annual conference foundation.

Church AI: Once each year, this flock holds a "What's Your Talent Harvest." Each member is encouraged to prepare something that uses his or her talent: woodworking, gardening, baking, art, yard maintenance, automotive repair, humorous speech-making, financial counseling, haircuts, dog washing, and so on. On "Harvest Day" these items (or proxies for services) are set up in the church parking lot and sold. (In the interest of full disclosure, I must mention that once when I was pastor I offered my cooking skills for auction to the highest bidder: I would prepare a meal for up to four people. The first bid was $15. I knew my culinary competence was recognized when the second bid was for $10.)

Church AJ: In this church of multiple adult Sunday school classes, the finance committee sent a representative to each class on "Stewardship Sunday" to present the church budget and to discuss biblical injunctions for giving. They reported that doing this in the smaller groups allowed for more freedom in the question and answer time.

Church AK: Leading up to the annual Commitment Sunday, each family was asked to have "family table time" to talk about the financial implication of Susanna Wesley's statement as she wrote about educating her children: "Religion is nothing else than doing the will of God, and not our own; that the one grand impediment to our temporal and eternal happiness being this self-will."

Church AL: Each time someone joins this congregation, he or she presents a pledge card as part of the service of reception. The amount, of course, is not revealed, but this public action reminds the entire congregation of how giving is part of the membership vow.

Church AM: One generous member of this church has agreed to anonymously match the funds raised for particular causes. Knowing that each dollar is going to become two dollars encourages others to give.

Church AN: In the new member class, this pastor always includes a discussion about sanctification and holy living. She raises the question: How do I know if my pocketbook has been sanctified?

Church AO: With a firm belief that fund-raising is rooted in prayer, this congregation has a twenty-four-hour prayer vigil before its financial campaign. For that entire period, there are at least two persons at the church building seeking the will of God and offering thanks for God's multiple blessings.

Church AP: The church has few members with regular incomes. Persons hesitate (or are unable) to commit to giving a certain amount to support the ministries. Some give prayer time. Some give volunteer time. Some give mission story-telling time. Some give vision-casting time. Some give witnessing time. One member responded to the challenge of giving $1,000 a year by saying: "I don't have $1,000, but I do have $20 each week. In a year's time, that makes up $1,000!"

Church AQ: This congregation was reluctant to have an Every Member Pledge campaign. Members did not want to sign up for a certain amount they would give. This made budget planning difficult, so the finance committee came up with this plan: On Commitment Sunday, members were given blank cards and without putting a name on the card, they turned in the cards with their estimate of their annual giving. (Most churches that ask for estimate of giving pledges assure the members they can change that amount at any time during the year if their circumstances change.)

Church AR: OK. This one is the church you are serving. What is its financial health, both in terms of resources for ministry and in terms of the spiritual discipline of stewardship? Maybe this could be on the agenda for the next church council meeting.

Here's an idea: Go back over these forty-four ideas and circle three that you will discuss with financial officers of your church.

Prayer: Good and generous God, with your own presence in our midst, you have taught us the power of sacrificial love. Help us learn what you have taught; help us live what you have lived. Amen.

Did you know that The United Methodist Church has an official teaching position that opposes gambling, including public raffles? (Look at ¶ 163 G in the Social Principles.) What is the implication of this for the local church that always draws names from the hat to determine the winners of the prizes given away at the annual community chicken dumplings supper? Is it gambling at a church party to say "Look under your chair and if there is an envelope taped there, you have won two tickets to the football game"? *The Book of Resolutions* (Resolution 4041) makes a statement first adopted in 1980 and endorsed by the General Conference as recently as 2016: "It is expected that United Methodist churches abstain from the use of raffles, lotteries, bingo, door prizes, other drawing schemes, and games of chance for the purpose of gambling or fund-raising." That doesn't give much wiggle room! But what are you to do if your congregation has a fifty-year tradition of raffling off a turkey at the annual Thanksgiving gala? A good first step is to find out if this is "just something we do" or is it a sacred cow for the congregation. If you feel the practice must be challenged (and you may not), start by alerting the church council to the official position of The United Methodist Church. Keep in mind that resolutions, even of the General Conference, are not part of "the law of the church." They are intended to be "instructive and persuasive," but they are not "command performance." The dialogue with the church council may or may not change plans for the next raffle. If not, then you face one of the most difficult of pastoral decisions: Is this worth fighting over? Is this worth risking the rest of my ministry? Answers do not come easily. Does it make a difference if the lottery is for a new car or if the lottery is just for a teddy bear? Does it make a difference if all the proceeds are going to a good cause? Instead of drawing a winning ticket out of a hat, how about giving the prize to the person who comes closest on a guess as to the number of marbles that fill a big glass jar? Does it matter if the raffle is just for fun or if it is a key component in raising funds for mission?

So, what's the big deal? With major moral and ethical issues swirling all around us, why take time to ponder drawing names out of a hat? Do you agree with this claim made in Resolution 4041 in *The Book of Resolutions*: "Gambling feeds on human greed and invites persons to place their trust in possessions rather than in God"? Do you think this conversation about church raffles is making a mountain out of a molehill? Do you resist even "low-level gambling" because it creates a dangerous environment for those with a gambling addiction? Do you see this as a no harm, no foul situation? Your decision here probably should not come easily! I think the person was wrong who told you that pastoral ministry was a cakewalk. Oops. Is a cakewalk considered gambling?

Kenneth Fisher called his neighboring pastor, Jeremy Baum. "I've just got to vent!" "What happened?" "Well, last Sunday we had the baptism of a baby." "Good. Infant baptism is a good thing. Did something go wrong?" "For starters, the parents sent out invitations inviting friends and family to come to little Egbert's christening." "Christening?" "Heavens, yes! Calling baptism 'christening' is substituting the part for the whole. Grrr!" "Yeah, christening is just about the name, but baptism is a lot more than that!" "I'm just getting warmed up. Just as I got ready to dip my hand into the water and get a good handful, Egbert's mom handed me a rose. She wanted me to sprinkle the kid with the rose. I suppose she wanted me to use as little water as possible." "I see what you mean. The rose becomes the symbol rather than the water." "You got that right. I suppose the Lord is able to deal with our mess ups, but I surely have a lot of teaching to do." "Uh, Ken, would you like to meet for a cup of coffee? I have the feeling you still have some venting to do!"

Baptism

Even though baptism has been pivotal in the experience of the Christian church from the command of Jesus (Matthew 28:19) to the practice of the early apostles (Acts 8:12) to the baptism of entire households, including children (Acts 16:15) to the teaching of Paul (Romans 6:3) to the oneness of the body of Christ (1 Corinthians 12:13) to the reality in the early church (Galatians 3:27), today's Christians do not agree on the purpose, mode, meaning or sign of this sacrament. In 1996 (and every quadrennium since), the General Conference adopted a report from a Baptism Study Committee: *By Water and the Spirit: A United Methodist Understanding of Baptism*. It can be found in several places: electronic copy at umcdiscipleship.org or umc.org/what-we-believe or in print form in *The Book of Resolutions* (8031, pp. 706–25) ordered from online sources. Other good places for your study include "Services of the Baptismal Covenant" (p. 81, *The United Methodist Book of Worship*), Article XVII of The Articles of Religion of The Methodist Church (¶ 104), and Article VI of The Confession of Faith of the Evangelical United Brethren Church (¶ 104).

These resources underline the emphasis on baptism as a sign of what God has done, what God is doing, and what God will do. "A Service of Death and Resurrection" includes these opening words: "As in baptism [*Name*] put on Christ, so in Christ may [*Name*] be clothed with glory." Baptism is a sign of God's "forever claim" upon us, both in life and in death.

Baptism makes a person a member of the church. (Remember the difference between baptized member and professing member? Check back on p. 46 for the discussion about these terms.) Because baptism is as reliable as God's promises, one is baptized only once. In fact, *The Book of Discipline* (¶ 341.7) could not be more clear: "No pastor shall re-baptize. The practice of re-baptism does not conform to God's action in baptism and is not consistent with Wesleyan tradition and the historic teaching of the church. Therefore, the pastor should counsel any person seeking re-baptism to participate in a rite of reaffirmation of baptismal vows." (See "The Baptismal Covenant IV" in *The United Methodist Hymnal*. It is a service for congregational reaffirmation of the baptismal covenant. The other services for baptism also usually include this component.) United Methodists recognize any Trinitarian baptism administered with water by an authorized person (¶¶ 129, 225). Some traditions only practice believer's baptism, at which time the person being baptized makes a profession of faith. In The United Methodist Church, such a baptism is recognized, although the traditional pattern is infant baptism. Persons who are baptized before they are able to answer for themselves are to be nurtured to make a profession of faith (a confirmation by the Holy Spirit of the baptismal vows). Persons who are able to answer for themselves when baptized are not expected to have a separate ritual for confirmation.

Most clergy have solid biblical and theological understandings of this sacrament. The difficulties emerge, so to speak, in the small print. Let's dialogue a bit about some of the sticky points related to baptism.

What is the appropriate mode of baptism? United Methodists practice all three traditional modes of Christian baptism: sprinkling, pouring, or immersion. Water is such an important symbol for washing away sin (Hebrews 10:22) that we dare not skimp on its use. If sprinkling, use enough water to let it be seen and felt. Pouring is just what it sounds like: water from a pitcher is poured over the head of the person being baptized.

(Their head is often positioned over a basin.) If there is a request for immersion (totally submerged in the water), some pastors have found a nearby body of water (a lake or the flowing water of a river); some have brought a large tub into the worship space; others have found a neighboring church (often Baptist) that would open its baptistery for United Methodist use. (I have found that Baptist clergy friends have been willing to loan me waders to use for these services.)

Where do you get the water? There is something powerful about using ordinary water from the ordinary faucets at the church or homes. God does great things with the ordinary things of life (John 1:14)! Sometimes, persons want to add water from the Jordan River in the Holy Lands or use water from some locale that has particular family meaning. That is acceptable, but be careful not to suggest that this is somehow more "magical" or "spiritual" than spigot water. Be sure to double-check the font or basin or pitcher to be certain there is water actually there. (One of my favorite baptism accounts is of the pastor who discovered at the critical moment in the service that there was no water in the baptismal font. He quickly said "Let us pray." While he led an extemporaneous prayer he took advantage of the fact that everyone had eyes closed. The brother reached over and emptied the water from the nearby flower vase into the font. Problem solved!) Among the strong water images in the Bible are Revelation 7:17, Acts 8:36, John 7:38, John 4:14, Zechariah 14:8, Jeremiah 17:13, Song of Solomon 4:15, Psalm 65:9, Psalm 23:2.

Who can administer baptism? In The United Methodist Church, an elder in full connection can baptize, although those on honorable location (¶ 358.2) and those on administrative location (¶ 359.3) and those who are on voluntary leave of absence (¶ 353.8) are limited to the place where they have put their charge conference membership. In addition, provisional elders and local pastors may conduct baptisms "within and while appointed to a particular charge or extension ministry" (¶ 316.1). There is a classic understanding that some traditions honor that in an absolute emergency anyone can baptize.

Where can a baptism take place? The question might well be not so much "where" but "with whom"? Paragraph 224 of *The Book of Discipline* sees the norm as the gathered congregation. If for whatever "good reason" this is not possible, the pastor should see that representative laypersons are there in behalf of the congregation. Further, if the baptism occurs in a community other than the one in which the person lives, the pastor is to make sure that the district superintendent or pastor in that person's home area shall be notified (¶ 226.2c).

What do I do with the water after the baptism? If the unused bread and grape juice from a Communion service is consumed or reverently poured back into the ground from which it has come, perhaps some care should also be given to the water left in the font or basin after a baptism. In some churches, the water remains in the font as a sign of expectancy of other baptisms and as a reminder of earlier baptisms. Other churches may have a tradition of emptying the font/basin into the ground. Some pastors save some of the water in a bottle that is given to the family of the baptized as a reminder of the sacramental occasion. Some congregations have a tradition of placing the water at the exit so persons might touch it as they leave, thus remembering their own baptism.

Here's an idea: Encourage parents to celebrate the anniversary of their child's baptism; there is no reason ever to stop those celebrations; it plants good seeds in the child's memory! Send a reminder card on the first anniversary of the baptism.

Prayer: Life-giving, nourishing God, thank you for the water-washed new beginning you give us in our baptism. Amen.

Marilyn Yow and J. R. Caviness sat, waiting for the concert to begin. Longtime friends, they had bought tickets for this special night out: no studies, no visits, no planning, no calls—just an evening of relaxation and restoration. "I know we promised not to talk 'business' tonight," J. R. began, "but I'm excited. I'm doing my first wedding this weekend."

Wedding

Provisional elders and local pastors can be approved annually to be licensed to preside at a service of marriage if state law allows (¶ 316). This authority is limited to the charge or extension ministry to which one is appointed. *The Book of Discipline* spells out what that means: "The charge or extension ministry will be defined as 'people within or related to the community or ministry setting being served.'" Some states will recognize the right to do marriage ceremonies by anyone whom the denomination recognizes. Some states require that persons doing weddings be bonded. Some states insist on ordination. Some states . . . well, you get the idea; you best check with local authorities.

It is up to you to decide whether or not you perform the ceremony—¶ 340.2a(3)(a). (Some have argued that civil law might override this provision.) You are expected to provide counseling with the parties involved. Some pastors find that these premarital sessions with the couple go more helpfully if they begin by planning together the wedding service. Going through the ceremony (nos. 864–69 in *The United Methodist Hymnal*) will engage many of the important issues to be discussed. (For example, what does it mean to "gather in the sight of God"? Why are the vows made in the presence of witnesses? What does it mean to "unite their families"? Which of the vows is going to be the most difficult to keep? How do the rings signify the union between Christ and his church? In what way is a marriage a covenant?) You have veto power over any ingredients the couple wants to use in the ceremony. If they want to write their own vows, make sure they are appropriate for the context of Christian worship. The service as laid out in *The United Methodist Hymnal* offers flexibility for various situations, but a look at that ritual is a good place to start. Reviewing the Social Principles on Marriage, Single Persons, and Women and Men, (¶ 161 C, E, F) is also helpful.

It is possible, but not likely, that the couple will, after counseling, decide to postpone or to call off the wedding. (I have conducted 113 marriage ceremonies; only once did the man and woman decide to cancel their plans to get married.) Obviously, there is some judgment call as to how much and how extensively you counsel with the potential husband

and wife. Some circumstances do not allow for the ideal arrangements for counseling. As is true for all counseling, these occasions are confidential (¶ 341.5).

These pre-wedding conversations are a time for some frank, even embarrassing, talk. What sexual attitudes does each party have? How do they feel about money management? Have they given thought to having/ not having children? How do their families get along? What does each see as the ideal living condition? What role will church-life and faith experience have in the marriage?

Some pastors have used personality inventories to help the individuals to get to know themselves and the other in a more insightful way. These tools can certainly get a good conversation started. (You might do an internet search for behavioral style analysis to find some possible instruments. One that is often used is Taylor-Johnson Temperament Analysis.).

If the man and woman have already been living together you may wish to talk about that. (Some pastors—by no means all—require such a couple to live apart for a few months prior to the wedding.) If either or both parties have previously been married, those circumstances need to be part of the dialogue.

Make sure the couple understands their legal obligations. Some states insist on a medical exam. Some states require the marriage to be in the same county where the license is obtained. Some states have requirements about the age of the official witnesses.

If the wedding is at the church, are there building-use policies in effect? Are there fees involved? A wedding director (provided either by the church or by the couple) can be a big help in getting folks in and out, getting folks seated, and having people in the right place at the right time. Keep in mind that the Service of Christian Marriage is a worship service and you are the responsible leader. For example, you may want to make sure that photographers know the policy about flash photography and the understanding about where they can move about during the ceremony. Use your own judgment about participation in the reception that may follow the service. To fail to attend may be seen as an insult to the couple.

Be aware that the present language of *The Book of Discipline* prohibits United Methodist clergy from conducting "ceremonies that celebrate homosexual unions" (¶ 341.6). Additionally, performing same-sex wedding ceremonies is a chargeable offense (¶ 2702.1b). Choosing to violate these provisions is a conscience-driven decision that some pastors make. Such a choice should be made in full awareness of the possible consequences for one's ministry. (While you are in the neighborhood, look at ¶ 341 for seven things listed as "unauthorized conduct" for pastors.)

Here's an idea: Get the church council to establish policies about the use of the church building for weddings, noting such matters as fees, rearranging worship space furniture, photography, use of outside pastors, arrangements for clean-up, and so on.

Prayer: Creator God, the Author of love, bring your Spirit into our love for one another that we may give glory to you in the way we love. Amen.

Miscellaneous

Here is a brief break in the flow of this book to mention a few things that have not seemed to fit in anywhere else!

Can I wear a stole? Traditionally, the stole is a sign of ordination, either as a deacon or as an elder. Some annual conferences—but not all—allow anyone (including local pastors) who is authorized for Word and Sacrament to wear a stole. In *The United Methodist Book of Worship*, the service for ordination includes provision of presentation of a stole (684), while the service for presenting licenses to local pastors does not (717).

What about my pension? Plans for pension benefits vary from annual conference to annual conference (¶ 1506.1). For example, in some annual conferences full-time local pastors are eligible for pension benefits but not part-time. In other annual conferences, part-time clergy are eligible. The pension status for those in extension ministries may vary. Each annual conference has its own plan to cover benefits for service prior to 1982. Individuals have choices to make about their own contributions to a pension program and have to make decisions about how to invest their funds. You should not be surprised now to see that my best recommendation is for you to contact your annual conference benefits officer to get the lay of the land where you are. This person is sometimes part of the office of the conference treasurer. There is a denomination-wide general agency regarding pensions and investments and you might get information from them (wespath.com), but your specific data will need to come from your own annual conference.

Who stores what where when? If that question makes no sense to you, be grateful. It means you have not run into this problem! The issue emerges when there is a furnished parsonage and the incoming pastor also has a houseful of furniture. Some annual conferences have tried to resolve the matter by having parsonage policies that indicate what will be left unfurnished in a parsonage (typically, a bedroom and a den). In some annual conferences, a pastor may live in his or her own housing (even if a parsonage is available) provided it is approved by the Pastor-Parish Relations Committee, charge conference, district superintendent, and the bishop's cabinet. In such a case, because there is a parsonage available there is no remuneration for the pastor. (You can probably find such parsonage guidelines on your conference website.) But, if you want to put your furniture in the parsonage, who is billed for storing the parsonage furniture? If you want to use the parsonage furniture, who is responsible for storing your personal belongings? You will need to negotiate this with the trustees or parsonage committee; but, in the final analysis, the burden is probably going to fall to you.

Commercial storage unit? Renting out your own furnished house while you are in parsonage? Unused room at the church? Storage space in a member's house? Empty room or basement at the parsonage? Sell your furniture or donate it to charity? Keep your furnished house as a "second home"? Make the front lawn of the parsonage look like a junk yard? (Not my best suggestion.) Split arrangements with the church, storing some of your stuff and storing some of the personage furnishings? Now, do you see why I said you should be grateful if this is not an issue for you! (One pastor reported that his predecessor had stored personal belongings in the parsonage basement; he wanted to leave them there "for a while," even after the new pastor moved in. Are we having fun yet?)

What if I am no good at counseling? Our spiritual gifts do vary. Note the word in Ephesians 4:11 is "some," not "all." I recall how my seminary course in pastoral counseling began. The professor walked through the door, strode to the podium, and with no introduction or greeting, said simply, "Know when to refer." Consult with colleagues about good places to refer those matters that put you into deep waters. One of your responsibilities is "to counsel persons with personal, ethical, or spiritual struggles" (¶340.2a[2]) Immerse these conversations in prayer. Listen more than you talk. Hear the story behind the story. Keep confidences. Wonder what you are not hearing about. Perhaps share your insights as questions, not answers. Comfort with reality, not just pie in the sky. Confront with caring and grace. And, know when to refer!

What help is available for my local church leaders? In addition to district and annual conference events, you might obtain some of the official resources such as *Church Financial Records Handbook* and *Church Membership Records Manual*. Also available in electronic or print form is a series called "Guidelines for Leading Your Congregation." You can order a full set or secure individual materials in English, Spanish, and Korean for subjects such as Trustees, Stewardship, Finance, Men's Ministries, Women's Ministries, various age levels, scouting and civic youth-serving ministries, Church Council, Communications, Lay Leader/Lay Member of Annual Conference, Nominations and Leadership Development, Pastor-Parish Relations, Evangelism, Mission, Small Group Ministries, Pastor, Small Membership Church, Church Historian, Family Ministries, Higher Education and Campus Ministry, Church and Society, and Worship. Look for these resources at Cokesbury.com.

Should I put my sermons on the internet? Having audio or written forms of sermons can be a gift to shut-ins or those who have to miss a week or two. Some church websites carry the full service live or recorded. Some congregations have a plan for recording the service and then have lay volunteers take it to share with the homebound. Be careful if you have, uh, borrowed generously from another preacher; I think there is a not-very-nice word for claiming something is yours when it really isn't. And, be prepared for an eventual ego-controlling message from some church you have served. Some years after I had moved from a pastoral appointment, I was contacted by a staff member at that church. "Would you like some of the cassette tapes of the sermons you preached while you were here?" I declined because I had one or two and figured that was enough. Then came the closer. The staff member said, "We were just getting ready to throw them all away and thought we'd see if you wanted any of them." Oh, well.

What has five eyes and is always wet? Mississippi River. (Feel free to use that on some nearby young child.) The point here is not really on "i's" but on "eyes," as in "four are better than two." Is there a volunteer, a spouse, a youth, a teacher, someone who doesn't like you—someone who can proofread the bulletin before you make copies or can look over the material you plan to have projected next Sunday? The internet has all sorts of examples of snafus and boo-boos from bulletins. Looking over what you have prepared might even be a ministry that a home-bound member could offer. Of course, having an error-free bulletin takes away one of the entertainment features for folks who get bored during your sermon.

What do you do about a colleague who seems to have run off the rails? First, do nothing. Your observation may be based on some rare circumstance or a misperception of a situation. Then, double-check your own heart. Is this simply a matter of disagreeing on ministry priorities or political views or previous "bad blood"? Double-check your motives. If you continue to feel that your pastor friend is in jeopardy of self-wounding or has done damage to the gospel message or has lapsed into irrational behavior or has some inappropriate relationship, spend a season in prayer. If the Spirit pushes you on in this awareness, arrange to speak with this colleague. Be aware that this could put any future ties at risk. Maybe you could be prepared to direct your friend to some trustworthy sources of help. (Does your annual conference provide confidential counseling services?) If this does not lead to a new and better direction, consult with someone else who, in a nonjudgmental way, can confirm that your observations have been seen by others. Maybe two or three pastoral colleagues could have an "intervention." (If this is a new concept for you, read about it on some Alcoholics Anonymous site.) If you see your colleague continue to self-destruct, get in touch with the district superintendent. The speed at which you go through these steps depends on the nature of your relationship, the seriousness of the occurrences, and the clarity of the God-led presence. Emergencies call for immediate action; slow-simmering matters may take a different pace.

What about your personal time/family time? Jesus kept a rhythm between his work and his time apart (for example, Luke 4:42, 6:12, 9:10, 9:18). It is not easy to do. Do you remember how the crowds sometimes interrupted Jesus in those times apart? You have your own pressures pushing against your having a balanced life. Studies. Pastoral duties. Unexpected crises. Spiritual drought. Spouse work schedule. Finances. Silly clock with only twenty-four hours in a day. Some annual conferences have a vacation policy, recommending "time away," depending on clergy status and years of service. (If so, it is probably on your annual conference website.) What recharges your batteries—an out-of-town shopping trip? A big league ball game? A silent retreat? Sleeping late? A blitz of movies? Visit to the university library? Joining a bowling league? Tent camping? A weekend at the beach? Two weeks in the mountains? Obviously, different strokes for different folks.

One of the best vacations my wife and I had was one we decided not to plan. At every major intersection, we took turns deciding which way to go. We ended up in a major city downtown traffic snarl; we came upon a previously unvisited national landmark; we passed buffalo in a huge pasture; we ended up in a small town and watched the local Little Theatre group perform the musical *Fiddler on the Roof.* That was just the first day! Keep in mind that unless your time apart includes some time apart from Sunday responsibilities, it may not give the Holy Spirit room to touch new places in your journey. (Life will go on at the church! Colleague to cover emergency pastoral care? Music Sunday? Retired pastor to preach? Lay speaker? Youth Sunday? Associate pastor who does not get many chances to preach? Conference staff? Clergy in extension ministry, such as a hospital chaplain or a professor or a counselor or a nonprofit worker? Leave a video of you preaching? Colleague on medical leave? District officer for United Methodist Women, United Methodist Men, or United Methodist Youth? Someone who owes you a favor?) When you leave to get away, leave your guilt about it at the backdoor. Who knows—it might wander off while you are gone.

Here's an idea: As you journey through this year of clergy life, make a few notes of "things I wish I had known." Send a note to The General Board of Higher Education and Ministry's Office of Clergy Formation (gbhem.org) and encourage those items to be added to licensing or orientation programs.

Prayer: Savior God, who led a people across the wilderness to a promised land, I thank you for your presence during the uncertain days of my own experience. Amen.

The First Firsts

Imani Petteway and Teresa Cobb sat next to each other at annual conference. This was the first time they had attended as clergy, both serving as full-time local pastors. It was the year for election of delegates to General Conference. "I know we can't vote for delegates to General Conference because we are local pastors, not members in full connection," Teresa said. "Yeah, but look over there at Fred Fox; he surely is planning to vote; in fact, he told me whom he was going to vote for. Isn't he a local pastor?" "Mutter mutter," muttered Imani.

General Conference

This conversation opens up about 3,412 questions. Let's deal with a few of them here.

Who can vote for delegates to General Conference? Let's start with the question stirred in the conversation above. Lay members of the annual conference vote for lay delegates to General Conference. Some clergy members can vote for the clergy delegates to General Conference. Prior to 2008, only clergy in full connection could vote for clergy delegates, but since a 2008 constitutional amendment was approved, some local pastors and provisional members are eligible to vote. Paragraph 35 of the Constitution grants that right to clergy members in full connection, to associate members, to provisional members who have completed all educational requirements, and to local pastors who have served under appointment for two consecutive years immediately before the election and who have completed either an M.Div. degree or have completed the Course of Study. It is easy to see why Teresa and Imani were confused when they saw one of their local pastor colleagues engaged in voting for delegates to General

Conference. Only elders and deacons are eligible for election, but *some* local pastors and provisional members can also vote. Some see that the distinction is historically rooted in the security of appointments for those elders in full connection (¶ 334.1), which is given in conjunction with the elder's promise to go where sent (¶ 334.2a). This discussion will continue in future General Conference decision-making.

What is the General Conference? Now, let's come back to the basic question. It takes the Constitution four articles to answer this question (¶¶ 13–16), and let it be noted, that one of the articles has sixteen sub-paragraphs. In addition, *The Book of Discipline* spells out the implications of the Constitution, with ¶¶ 502–11 giving details about composition, presiding officers, rules of order, quorum, and petitions. (Perhaps you can set these paragraphs to music and have them sung as a seasonal cantata. Perhaps not.) It boils down to this: General Conference is a delegated legislative body of United Methodists from throughout the world (right now about 60 percent from the United States). It is the only group that can speak in the name of The United Methodist Church (¶ 509). Any United Methodist organization (that includes the youth Sunday school class) and any clergy member of The United Methodist Church (that probably includes you) and any lay member of The United Methodist Church (that includes your strong-minded Uncle Bert) can petition the General Conference to take action, including making changes in *The Book of Discipline* (¶ 507). The General Conference has "full legislative power over all matters distinctively connectional" (¶¶ 16, 501). One slightly skewed way of saying that is that the General Conference writes *The Book of Discipline*. Constitutional changes require annual conference votes (¶ 59); General Conference actions are subject to an appeal to the Judicial Council regarding their constitutionality (¶ 56). Unless called into special session (¶ 14), the General Conference meets every four years.

Who are these people? Half of the delegates to General Conference are laity and half are clergy. Elders and deacons are the only clergy eligible to be elected (¶ 35.) Each annual conference (or missionary conference or provisional conference) elects a number of delegates based on a formula that includes both the number of clergy in that annual conference and the number of lay members (¶¶ 502.2, 511.5). The total delegate count is between 600 and 1,000—¶ 13. In addition, The United Methodist Church has a concordat (covenant) relationship with The Methodist Church of Great Britain (4), The Methodist Church of the Caribbean/the Americas (2), The Methodist Church of Mexico (2), and The Methodist Church of Puerto Rico (2). These groups also have delegates as noted. At the 2016 General Conference, the official languages (for which translators were provided) were English, French, Korean, Portuguese, Spanish, and Kiswahili.

How does General Conference work? Some longtime delegates might answer that: "Sleep deprivation." Proposed legislation—all those petitions filed by United Methodists around the world, including church agencies—are assigned to a legislative committee that makes a recommendation to the full General Conference regarding the petition: accept (concur), deny (do not concur), amend. After getting this recommendation, the full General Conference makes the final decision. In some way, every single one of those petitions (often over ten thousand) is considered. In 2016, the legislative committees were Church and Society, Conferences, Discipleship, Faith and Order, Financial Administration, General Administration, Global Ministries, Independent Commissions, Judicial Administration, Local Church, and Ministry and Higher Education/Superintendency. Because central conferences (those outside the United States) have some prerogative to adjust administrative rules to fit local settings (¶ 31.5), there is also a standing Committee on Central Conference Matters.

What difference does this make to the local church? The first response is that the local church is accountable to the language of *The Book of Discipline*. [For example, some items use "shall" language—no choice, and other items use "may" language (choice), or "recommend" language (encouraged, but not required)]. And, of course, your status and authority as a clergy member is subject to General Conference action. Of import to the local church is the authority of the General Conference to provide and revise the denominational official worship resources, such as hymnals. Each local congregation is directly impacted by the General Conference's constitutional power to raise funds for the work of the church—apportionments (¶ 16.9). Particularly through the Social Principles (¶¶ 160–66), the General Conference speaks as The United Methodist Church to individuals, local churches, and to the world. In an effort to make General

Conference meetings accessible to members throughout the connection, the site of the General Conference has been rotated among the five geographic jurisdictions in the United States and, in the future, areas outside the United States. Get up a busload or a plane load? (2004—Pittsburgh; 2008—Fort Worth; 2012—Tampa; 2016—Portland, Oregon; 2019—St. Louis (called session); 2020—Minneapolis; 2024—Manila, Philippines; 2028—Harare, Zimbabwe.)

What do you do if you disagree with the General Conference? The answer to this depends on the basis for your disagreement, the intensity of your disagreement, and your willingness to accept the consequences of the disagreement. One thing you can do is to begin working on a petition to the next General Conference to make a change that seems right to you. Talk to members of your delegation to General Conference and keep them informed on your opinion. Paragraph 164 F from the Social Principles discusses civil disobedience and notes that part of this conscience-driven response includes "being willing to accept the costs of disobedience." This is no less true with the church's understanding of accountability. As a pastor in The United Methodist Church, you have the responsibility to identify and share the official denominational position on a matter; then, if you disagree, you can continue by saying "Here are reasons I do not agree with this position."

 Here's an idea: Host a speaker from your annual conference delegation to General Conference and invite other congregations to join you.

Prayer: Holy Trinity, you show us in your divine oneness the power of one life together; grant us such grace that we might live in healthy unity. Amen.

Two laypeople from Barber Heights United Methodist Church had decided to observe some of the annual conference session. They were not members of the annual conference, but simply wanted to see how the annual conference worked. After sitting through the election of delegates to General Conference, one said to the other, "Why are they still voting? I thought they elected everybody they needed to." "Evidently not," came the answer, "because now they are voting on delegates to the jurisdictional conference."

Council of Bishops

Jurisdictions are large, geographic units of The United Methodist Church in the United States (North Central, Northeastern, South Central, Southeastern, and Western). Usually every four years (actually at the call of the Council of Bishops [¶ 26]), delegates from the annual conferences within that jurisdiction meet as a jurisdictional conference. (There can be special, called sessions, [¶ 521].) Although there are several "powers and duties" conferred to the jurisdictional conference (¶ 27), one that is singular is the election of bishops.

Important note: Outside the United States, these regional units are called central conferences (¶¶ 28–31). These are Africa Central Conference, Central and Southern Europe Central Conference, Congo Central Conference, Germany Central Conference, Northern Europe and Eurasia Central Conference, Philippines Central Conference, West Africa Central Conference. There are some differences between jurisdictional conferences and central conferences (e.g., time of meeting, bishops' term of office, adjusting the general *Discipline*), but explorations of those variances are beyond the scope of this book.

Each annual conference elects twice its number of General Conference delegates to be the delegates to its jurisdictional conference, continuing to maintain the equal number of lay and clergy delegates. Typically, this would be the delegation to General Conference plus an equal number chosen just for jurisdictional conference. Reserve delegates may also be elected. Eligibility to vote and eligibility to be elected are the same as for election to General Conference.

Bishops in the United States are elected for life (with mandatory retirement [¶ 408.1]). Their professing membership is not in a local church, but is in the Council of Bishops, even after retirement (¶ 422). When vacancies occur in the office of bishop (death, retirement, resignation, judicial procedure, leave of absence, medical leave), there are provisions for filling the vacancy (¶ 407), but most often the vacancy is filled by an election at the next jurisdictional conference.

There is a Jurisdictional Committee on Episcopacy—one layperson and one clergyperson from each annual conference—that recommends where bishops will be assigned (¶ 524.3b). The jurisdictional conference votes on those assignments. Bishops, like other clergy, are thus subject to a system of assignment.

The work of the jurisdictional conference directly impacts your local church. Program resources may be available. Financial support of institutions and agencies may be initiated. And it is at jurisdictional conference that it is determined who will be your bishop.

Here are some ruminations about the office of bishop.

- Bishops are human beings.
- Although in some predecessor bodies, district superintendents were elected, in The United Methodist Church they are elders appointed by the bishop as an extension of the superintending role of the bishop (¶¶ 53, 403.2).
- One of the Restrictive Rules in the Constitution says that the General Conference cannot do away with the episcopacy (¶ 19).
- How often you have face-to-face time with your bishop depends on the bishop's personal style and depends on the geography of your annual conference. (Some annual conferences are a portion of a state; others cover hundreds and hundreds of miles across state lines.) If you have a really special occasion in your local church, invite the bishop. (Some like these requests to come via the district superintendent.) The worst reply you can get is "You incompetent slob. Why don't you handle it yourself?" More likely, given enough notice, the answer will be "Let's see what we can work out."

- The New Testament word *episkopos* (usually translated "bishop") carries the implication of one who has oversight over a territory. Keep in mind that the bishop has to balance multiple dimensions of the church's life.
- Bishops are human beings.
- The Council of Bishops is established by the Constitution.
- The appointment-system is created by the Constitution (¶ 54).
- What you call the bishop varies a lot based on regional custom. Bishop Gregson might, in another part of the country, be known as Bishop Bob. Or maybe even just as Bob. Respect the office and take cues on what the bishop prefers. That seems to be the gracious thing to do.
- How much do bishops get paid? There are two answers: (1) not as much as you might think and (2) that figure is set by the General Conference. All bishops in the United States make the same salary.
- How can I find out how my bishop voted on the big issues at General Conference? You can't, because bishops do not have a vote at General Conference. Some of them will preside at plenary sessions but none of them has a vote.
- What if a bishop violates *The Book of Discipline*? The answer is a page long in *The Book of Discipline*, so check it out (¶ 2704.1).
- Does the bishop even know who I am? Hmmmm. Which way do you want it to be?
- Bishops are human beings.

Here's an idea: Look at important events that will be on your ministry-setting calendar two or three years from now. Plan with the church council about the possibility of inviting the bishop.

Prayer: Thank you, Lord of the church, for the ones set apart by your people to be our episcopal leaders. Bring Your Holy Spirit to them! Amen.

Harrill Miguel turned to his clergy neighbor, Jimmy Rhee, and asked, "What is this Judicial Council I keep reading about? Who are these people?" Pastor Rhee smiled and said, "I'm glad you asked. That's what we covered in polity class last week!"

Judicial Council

The Judicial Council, along with the General Conference and Council of Bishops, is one of the constitutional denomination-wide bodies (¶¶ 55–58). Sometimes, in shorthand terms it is described as the "Supreme Court" of The United Methodist Church. There are nine members, each elected by the General Conference. Every four years, it alternates between being majority lay (five out of nine) and being majority clergy (five out of nine) (¶ 2602.1). There are alternates, also elected by the General Conference, who serve in case a member has a conflict of interest, recuses for personal reasons, or is unable to attend or participate in a meeting. Unless an additional called session occurs, the Judicial Council meets twice a year. The members can come from throughout the worldwide church; the 2016–2020 Judicial Council has members from Liberia, Philippines, Mozambique, and Norway, as well as five who live now in the United States.

The work of the Judicial Council is important because its decisions are final (¶¶ 57, 2609.11), thus its determinations have implications for all United Methodists and United Methodist congregations. Those decisions can be seen at umc.org/who-we-are/judicial-council. Reviewing past decisions can help you see the breadth of the kinds of things that concern United Methodists.

The Judicial Council does not initiate the items that it considers. Certain bodies have the authority to ask for rulings on the constitutionality of proposed or completed legislation. They may ask for a declaratory decision as to the constitutionality, application, meaning, and effect of some portion of *The Book of Discipline*. They may appeal a bishop's decision of law. Except for persons asking for a review of an opinion or decision of a jurisdictional or central conference committee on appeals, individuals do not bring matters to the Judicial Council. (If this kind of work fascinates you, check out ¶¶ 2601–12. There is a lot in the "small print" that these broad statements do not cover.)

There are two ways in which the Judicial Council can change *The Book of Discipline*: (1) If something in the *Discipline* is ruled unconstitutional, that item is null, void, and of no effect. (2) If two paragraphs in *The Book of Discipline* appear to be in conflict, the Judicial Council can determine which one has precedence.

Here's an idea: Subscribe to the United Methodist News Service Daily Digest (umns.org) and get information on Judicial Council decisions and reports of United Methodist life around the world.

Prayer: Calm our spirits to receive your Spirit when we disagree; bring the freshness of your always current Word upon our decision-making. Amen.

Annual Conference

The Constitution says that "the annual conference is the basic body in the Church" (¶ 33). Constitutional amendments have to be approved by the total vote of all annual conferences. General and jurisdictional/central conference delegates are elected by the annual conference. Clergy members are approved by the annual conference. Ordination and licensing occurs through the annual conference.

To find contact information for your annual conference personnel, enter your annual conference name into an internet search. You might also find on that website resources for ministry, media center, youth programs, financial information, children's activities, music and worship materials, conference institutions, report policies and forms, information about upcoming meetings, continuing education opportunities, mission trips, older adult ministries, ideas that worked for other churches, and maybe—by hacking—the secret recipe for some congregation's famous apple butter.

The trust clause (¶ 2501) may lead some persons to say the annual conference owns your local church property. No, titles are held by your local church board of trustees. The trust clause is the reminder that "we are in this together." In a sense, it is a not-quite-accurate, but nevertheless helpful way of saying that each local church owns not only its building but also the building of the next United Methodist church down the road and the building of every United Methodist church six states away, and so on. It all "belongs" to all of us. Your local church holds its title, but it is in trust for all of us. Only if a local church were to separate from The United Methodist Church does its property become available for other United Methodist usages. This is nothing new. The concept emerged in the days of John Wesley and it has been in *The Book of Discipline* since 1797. Occasionally, the trust cause is tested in state courts, so if it is an issue, check it out with an attorney who understands United Methodist polity.

If you are serving as a licensed local pastor, your membership is in the annual conference (¶ 316.6). You can vote on all matters except constitutional amendments, election of delegates to General or jurisdictional conference, and matters of ordination, character, and conference relations of clergy. (That probably means that most years you can vote on 95 percent of the business of the annual conference.) Keep in mind that if you have completed your educational requirements and have served two consecutive years before the election, you may vote for clergy delegates to General and jurisdictional conferences.

From the time that Otterbein said to Boehm "*Wir sind Brüder*—We are brethren" . . . ever since Wesley called his preachers together . . . ever since Albright organized his connection . . . the United Methodist people have been conference. That is why there are lay and clergy *members* (not delegates) of an annual conference. That is the basic body.

Conclusion

Just before you move to your second appointment, you will find a few boxes that you never got around to unpacking. These pages have been devoted not to everything that a pastor needs to know and experience, but to those things you might need to know in order to get started. Some boxes you will not need. Some boxes should be opened first.

Let's take seriously 1 Peter 3:15: "Always be ready to make your defense to anyone who demands from you an accounting for the hope that is in you." Much of what United Methodists would say is affirmation is shared with almost all other Christians: salvation in and through Jesus Christ, the activity of the Holy Spirit, the universal church, the reign of God now and in the future, and the authority of Scripture. (Read more in ¶ 102.) But there are distinctive emphases in our tradition. To set them aside is to ignore a gift that God has given us to maintain.

One of those gifts is how we do theology. Scripture is primary. Tradition shows how God's truth has been present for others. Experience, both personal and corporate, is "confirmation of the realities of God's grace." Reason is a God-given instrument for clarity in communication. (See ¶ 105.)

The Book of Discipline notates several doctrinal accents in our heritage (¶ 102). Grace is the pervading theme. There is *prevenient grace*, the term we use to acknowledge that God always makes the first move in the divine encounter with us. *Justification* is pardon of sin, "getting right with God," and it too is a gift of grace. Ordinarily, those who receive this gift of faith are "assured" of their salvation. Then, there is the grace-gift of *sanctification* or holiness, holy living. We move toward the fullness of God's gift in Christian maturity (*perfection*), which is full love of God and full love of neighbor. Our traditions—both Methodists and Evangelical United Brethren before us—do not separate *faith* and *good works*. The good works are evidence of the faith that is at work within. Salvation moves us toward mission and service, personal piety, and social justice. The church provides both nurture for those in the fellowship and expressions of love of the neighbor.

These theological distinctions don't make us smarter or more holy or more scriptural or better than others. They do give us a particular lens through which to look at the gospel's encounter with the world. Why does God allow so many different viewpoints to exist within God's church? Maybe it is a reminder that God has more to give than will fit into any one box. But, if we fail to honor and proclaim what is in our box, that gift from God is lessened.

So, while you are deciding where that table ought to go, open up these biblical and theological boxes. God wants to use them and you are going to need them. And it will be a gift of life-giving grace.

CPSIA information can be obtained
at www.ICGtesting.com
Printed in the USA
LVHW091136130421
684340LV00012B/636